# Sacred Subversion

*How Some Churches*

*Defeat Pastors*

*and*

*Destroy Themselves*

Robert F. Simms

©2018 by Robert F. Simms.
All rights reserved. No part of this book may be reproduced, stored in a retrieval system, or transmitted in any form or by any means without the prior written permission of the publisher, except by a reviewer who may quote brief passages in a review to be printed in a newspaper, magazine, or journal.

ISBN: 978-0-9995929-1-5
PUBLISHED BY ROBERT F. SIMMS
Printed in the United States of America

# Contents

1 Shooting Straight............................ 7

2 Disrespecting the Pastor's Mission........... 14

3 The Double Standard........................ 38

4 Expecting Too Much......................... 54

5 Organizing for Failure...................... 73

6 The Church That Will Not Be Led,
  The Pastor Who Will Not Be Followed........ 97

7 Too Many Chiefs........................... 117

8 Hamstringing the Lead Sheep............... 130

9 Promulgating a Theology of Exaltation...... 142

10 Chronic Vexations......................... 158

11 Sacred Solutions.......................... 176

# 1

## Shooting Straight

**I have written to you quite boldly on some points, as if to remind you of them again, because of the grace God gave me to be a minister of Christ Jesus to the Gentiles with the priestly duty of proclaiming the gospel of God, so that the Gentiles might become an offering acceptable to God, sanctified by the Holy Spirit.**
**Romans 15:15-16, NIV**

This is not a gentle book. However, it isn't a mean book. It's simply an honest book, that shoots straight with the reader about the struggles many pastors and churches face, internal church problems that pastors discuss among themselves but rarely address their own congregations about. With frank descriptions of epidemic problems in churches everywhere, this book attempts to unmask the chief ways in which churches defeat their pastors, sometimes from the day they begin their ministries. These defeats are the harbingers of the implosion of many of these same churches, since undermining and subverting their pastors inevitably leads to the corruption of the church's very character and purpose.

*What is the Perspective?*

Up front, the author wishes to inform the reader preemptively of his first hand experience. I have spent more than twenty years in pastoral ministry and have had several painful experiences, including having been forced into resigning before securing another place of service. I have gone through crises involving a wide range of internal church problems, and have had conflicts with deacons and other groups or individuals who were insistent on imposing their will on the church and all its leaders. I am candid about my experience, and I describe this as preemptive information in order to answer the hasty dismissal of critics who might say my evaluation of the problems of churches is nothing more than scorning them for my own difficulties. No one, least of all me, would question the temptation of an oft-wounded man to rail on his assailants.

Indeed, bitterness has knocked at my door; and my experiences have resulted in my spending much time and thought evaluating what has taken place in my struggles. However, what God has done in my life through these crises has transformed me personally, reaching deeply into areas of my personality and character, causing me not only to understand many of the fundamental causes of church-pastor conflicts, but also to care about confronting these issues so that churches might change.

Furthermore, I write this book on the basis of many interviews with other pastors about their own experiences, and out of many conversations with denominational leaders who deal with church conflicts every day. From years of research—some of it academic, some of it informal—I have come to a conviction that churches simply must face their role in the crises that plague them.

## *What About Balance?*

Church members reading this book may question at this point why the book doesn't balance its critique of wayward church members with forceful rebuke of erring pastors. Don't some pastors need to change? Indeed, many authors have written with pastors in mind, helping them understand their problems with inappropriate or mismatched leadership styles, sins of poor time management, foolish counseling policies, and dozens of other things.

This book is addressed, however, to churches. For churches often blame pastors for the church's failure to grow, to recover from splits or losses from transition, or for the departure of members over miscellaneous matters. And while occasionally a pastor really did do something worthy of the sole blame, the story is usually more involved. Much of the time, church members with long track records of trouble making, axes to grind, or profoundly defective understanding of how biblical churches should function, are the key players in the failure of a pastorate or the downfall of a church.

Rarely can one leader destroy a church. Church members are deeply implicated in these distasteful dramas, and if the epidemic of church implosions and pastoral exits in Western culture is to be stemmed at all, church members on a wide scale must come to realize their central role in both the problems and the solutions.

## *What about the Approach?*

Since trying to open people's eyes to the depth of destructive behavior is my principal goal, one of the key questions for the author is what approach to take. The approach of this book, as we have already said, is not gentle. Some readers may describe it as blunt confrontation. Some may even think it too negative or discouraging.

The question is whether or not more diplomacy or even soft, positive reinforcement can deliver the message that desperately needs to be presented to the current generation of churches. Some people don't like anything but light, uplifting reading, just as they don't like anything but nice, gentle, mild-mannered preaching. Someone typified much preaching as "mild mannered men speaking in a mild mannered way to mild mannered people telling them how to be more mild mannered."[1] But there come times when mild, positive reinforcement is the least effective option among teaching methods. Occasionally the only thing that will awaken us to the monumental wrong in our own lives is to be shocked, stunned, and called to account.

The approach of this book will not be reviewed with praise or found palatable by some readers. But before rejecting its content, the reader is urged to do some sober thinking about far more important authors than this one,

---

[1] Attributed to Goodwin Hudson in an address to the World Congress on Evangelism in Berlin in 1966.

and far more powerful publishers than those that sell books to America and the world: the prophets of the Old Testament.

How blessed we are that Hosea, Joel, Amos, Malachi and others did not submit their works to be evaluated by people like those who told Isaiah, "Prophesy to us smooth things!" (Is. 30:10)! Even Isaiah and Jeremiah, whose works included entreaty, comfort and promise as part of their messages, also spent many pages laying out a bold, unapologetic, ungarnished confrontation of the sins of their hearers. They understood that people can come to a point in their sinful behavior at which they become inured to the suggestion that their hearts may be deeply sinful or that their behavior may be destroying their own lives. These prophets realized that sometimes only stark depictions inviting challenging encounters with naked truth can cut through self-deception and be heard by the soul.

How blessed we are, too, that Nathan did not come to King David saying, "Forgive me for bringing this up, Sire, but there is a matter I would suggest you address! And your lordship would be much happier if you were to, let us say, mend some fences in recognition that certain activities that took place in the past may have failed to be as admirable as they might have been." No! Nathan told a heart-wrenching tale featuring characters out of David's own pastoral upbringing, luring him to condemn the actions of some unknown perpetrator. Then Nathan pointed a bony finger into the face of the king and verbally slapped him in the face: "You are the man!" And he identified in no uncertain terms David's adultery and murder.

Practically every person reading these words, and who has ever learned any significant lesson in life, has had some encounter with brutal honesty that knocked out the props of complacency and self-deceit and struck home with life-changing force. Perhaps the fervent, frank assertions that follow on these pages will have a similar effect somewhere on someone, resulting in change.

This book, then, attempts to communicate hard truths to church members, with the hope that bluntness may result in opened eyes. Where offense is taken, it is my prayer that it may ultimately morph into truth realized.

*What about the Method?*

The method adopted for this quest involves both the topical outline of the book's chapters, and the biblical content of each one. I am and always have been devoted to the belief that God has provided all the necessary principles for teaching his covenant people in the pages of his divinely inspired book. In each chapter, I have attempted to describe various pastor-church conflicts in their true colors, and to illustrate from the experiences of persons whom I have known and from my own private saga.

Case studies are drawn mostly from my own family of the Christian faith, the circles of Southern Baptist churches. Understandably, I know more about my own denomination's churches. However, the crisis of church turmoil is decidedly universal among denominations. The ferment that feeds the church problems discussed in this book is spiritual in nature, not denominational, and is causing difficulties between ministers and memberships in churches of all stripes and polities.

Most of the case studies have also been disguised slightly to prevent identification of the actual churches and ministers involved. In some cases, names (or places, or other precise details) have been changed to protect the innocent. In other cases, they have been altered to mercifully spare the guilty.

After all, the purpose of the case studies and of the book as a whole is not to expose the identities of any persons or churches, but to expose the participants in similar real life dramas to the cutting edge of God's word.

Especially in churches whose confessions of faith is some sort of claim to believing that the Bible is their rule of faith and practice, it is time to listen to that word from God, to confess how it has been violated, and to submit to its instruction so that Christ, still using us, may build his church in our day.

# 2

# Disrespecting the Pastor's Mission

**My people come to you, as they usually do, and sit before you to listen to your words, but they do not put them into practice.**
**Ezekiel 33:31 NIV**

Most church members are clueless about the profound sense of calling that most pastor-preachers have. A preacher's experience of calling is often a dramatic event that changes the direction of his education or career. In some families of the Christian faith, one enters "the ministry" for the purpose of "helping people" or "serving the church." In the more evangelical church fellowships, one becomes a minister only if he feels "the call to preach," a deeply spiritual experience in which one senses the very voice of God, and comes to realize that for the rest of his life, he belongs to God in a unique way. It is this calling to "preach the word" (2 Tim. 4:2) that gives the pastor-preacher, and of course, evangelists, missionaries and preachers in any other setting, a profound conviction of their mission in life.

It is this calling, this sense of a personal assignment as a part of the great commission of Christ, that church members in general too often fail to comprehend. They may pay lip service to the pastor's calling, but too few grasp the power that this calling has over the minister himself, the sense of drive that it gives him, the hunger he has to fulfill it, and the grief he experiences every time his mission is thwarted by one of a thousand things. To put it simply:

***Because church members do not understand the pastor's calling, they frequently show disrespect for it and for him.***

This disrespect is not shown by any overt suggestion that the pastor's role is "just another job." Rather, it is demonstrated in the bafflingly casual way in which church members typically regard the sacred task of preaching, or the guiltless ease with which they excuse themselves from the disciplines the pastor—in his role of leading the church—charges them with adopting.

Two root problems emerge as the cause of this disrespect. One is a refusal to accept the concept and reality of what is called spiritual authority. The other is the failure to recognize that the pastor occupies an important place in that authority—by divine calling.

## Rejection of Spiritual Authority

A subject guaranteed to excite heated debate and loss of tempers among church members is the matter of spiritual authority. In American culture, in particular, the concept of there being persons in the church who have spiritual authority, and the implication that other persons are under that authority, is a recipe for rebellion. Yet the scripture clearly and repeatedly says that in the church, pastors (most often referred to as elders in the Bible) have such spiritual authority; and it is a church's rejection of this authority that constitutes the most significant root problem behind that church's disrespect for the preacher's mission. For the preacher's commission to "preach the word" directly implies that he delivers that word with the authority of the Lord. As Paul said to Timothy: "These things command and teach" (1 Tim. 4:11).

Indeed, without the spiritual authority the scriptures describe the preacher as having, his placement in the church as its main proclaimer and teacher would seem to have little purpose.

Hebrews contains some of the clearest language indicating the spiritual authority of pastors. In three verses in chapter 13, the author refers to "them that have the rule over you" (KJV). The NIV softens this translation considerably to "your leaders," a word which may mean anything from a tour guide to the President. But the Greek behind the English word(s) is not so flaccid.

The root Greek word in all three of those verses is ηεγεμονος (hegemonos) which means ruler or governor. It is the same word used in Luke 21:12, where Jesus said the disciples would be brought before "kings and rulers." It indicates authority, not merely inspirational leadership.

We should note carefully that the English word "hegemony" comes from this Greek root, and hegemony particularly means dominance, especially of one nation over another. There is nothing soft and fuzzy about the meaning of this word; and it is used to describe the spiritual leader of the church in his authoritative role.

Without digressing extensively to attempt to describe just how the New Testament elder or pastor was to "rule over" the church, we will acknowledge that whatever *hegemonos* meant, it was tempered by Peter's admonition to pastors: "not lording it over those entrusted to you, but being examples to the flock" (1 Peter 5:3, NIV).

Note the ends of the leadership spectrum: Peter warns pastors not to play "Lord" over the church (employing a Greek word based on κυριος, the word used for Jesus as "Lord.") But Hebrews 13:17 speaks of pastors (elders) as "them that have the rule over you," and then instructs church members to "submit yourselves." The NIV even adds, "to their authority."

Putting the two counterpoint instructions together, we may draw the conclusion that somewhere between the merely inspirational example of a figurehead who has no actual authority, and the ultimate Lordship of Christ who has all authority (Mat. 28:18), lies the spiritual authority of pastors. In the church, the sphere for their exercise of that authority, the Bible accords them the right to give direction. By implication as well as by explicit direction, the Bible instructs church members to respect pastoral leadership and to follow it.

This instruction has implications that seem like a can of worms for congregationally governed churches (such as Baptists). Over generations, the theory of congregational government has evolved to an almost exclusively democratic model. Yet, the Bible clearly vests in the "elders" (pastors and, in New Testament churches, apparently multiple pastors or elders) authority to lead that the democratic model eliminates by design. Every generation that passes without our dealing with the discrepancies of this system of governance brings us more and more problems stemming from church-pastor conflicts, many of which are solely about who has the authority to lead the church.

Let's be honest about how the problem has developed. Overwhelmingly, it is congregations that wrest control from their leaders, not leaders who surrender their leadership role to congregations. While certainly there are ministers who are less enthusiastic about making decisions than others, it is part of the role of the pastor to give direction. Few pastors could be found who would be able to maintain convincingly that they don't mind not having any executive role.

Who or what is at fault for churches refusing to honor the God-given, Bible-based authority of their pastors?

*The Demise of Church Discipline*

Certainly part of the reason is to be found in the disappearance of church discipline in most congregations. Here at the turn of the twenty-first century, many of the older generation can still remember times when congregations of their youth "churched" a member—an ironic euphemism for voting to remove a member for some sin. Farther back into the twentieth century and before, churches wielded their authority to act in numerous other disciplinary ways toward erring members. Churches attempted to put into practice various, and somewhat ambiguous references by the Apostle Paul or Jesus to disciplining believers.

- Persons "delivered to Satan" (1 Cor. 5:5, 1 Tim. 1:20)
- Persons receiving "punishment...inflicted by many" (2 Cor. 2:6)
- Hypocritical brethren: "with such an one, no not to eat" (1 Cor. 5:11)
- Members disobeying apostolic direction: "have no company with him ...yet count him not as an enemy, but admonish him as a brother" (2 Thes. 3:14-15)
- Trespassers: "If he neglect to hear the church, let him be unto thee as an heathen man and a publican."

Whatever forms these instances of church discipline took, they clearly used public disapproval or disavowal of the member, or even removal of the person from the church's fellowship.

In previous generations, discipline fitting into the foregoing pattern often was effective because Christians valued their being in the church, their ability to attend worship, and their acceptance in communities that were heavily dominated by the church's congregation. Indeed, an individual Christian's ability to interact with a community sometimes depended on his being right with the church.

What changed this intrinsic authority in the church? In great part, the change resulted from the decline in the church's great influence in communities. In general, neither Catholic nor Protestant churches wield the kind of power of example or leadership over their communities that they did fifty or a hundred years ago. Some of this decline is due to lower ratios of Christians to non-Christians. But much of it can be laid at the doorstep of social revolution—a rejection of all authority to some degree, and a rejection of religious authority to a great degree.

While church discipline historically has been a function of the church as a whole, not pastors acting alone, the rejection of spiritual authority has focused not simply on congregational actions, but on the position of pastors, in particular.

There was a time when pastors were widely and highly respected community leaders, in communities of all sizes. Discussions of "the way things used to be" usually yield the impression that the respect accorded pastors (and by extension, their churches) was genuine. The membership of many civic and political leaders in churches accounted for some of this respect. But even among many non-church-going leaders, an odd, perhaps never-to-be repeated sense of honor pervaded much of American culture for the church as an institution. In many small towns in the southern United States, pastors still experience some of that honor. But across the nation and throughout western culture, the honor accorded the church has seriously eroded.

With the erosion of the society's respect of the church has come the erosion of churches' respect of their pastors. After all, church members are part of the culture, too. Even pastors, in general, do not take seriously enough the importance of their exercising biblical authority in their congregations. Many are content to be figureheads, and they hold out the hope that merely by their example and by urging opinions and convictions from the pulpit they can move their churches to make the right congregational decisions.

Much of pastors' adoption of this toothless view of their role, however, is the result of defeat. Overwhelmed by the tide of disrespect and individualism in the culture and the church, pastors have conceded the ground on which they once stood as leaders with authority. They have magnified the servant model of leadership found in the Bible until it eclipses the role of prophet or elder, and with this new theology to baptize their surrender, they have become docile participants in the demolition of an important part of their own calling.

*Inadequate Preaching and Teaching*

Sensibility dictates that individual pastors should not be held accountable for the tsunami of cultural rejection of their spiritual authority. However, pastors in general have not sufficiently taught the biblical model of spiritual authority in the church.

Denominations certainly bear some guilt for this failure. For instance, Southern Baptists as a denomination have championed the ideas of individual autonomy and church autonomy. Insofar as individual autonomy means a person may read and interpret the Bible for himself and needs no intermediary between himself and God but Jesus Christ, this idea is thoroughly biblical. And insofar as church autonomy means that there is no human, religious hierarchy with any authority over the local church, this idea, too, is biblical.

Unfortunately, the general trend in churches for the past several generations has been toward the tyranny of unbridled democracy, the idea that no pastor they call will be able to do anything in an executive fashion, but that every matter will come before the church for a vote, and usually that every matter will go through the deacons first. In spite of the fervent belief of many congregational churches, such as Baptists, that this democratic ideal is the divinely ordered scheme of things, it cannot be found in the Bible. And Baptists long ago declared the Bible to be their rule of faith and practice. What has gone wrong?

Indeed, the Bible does teach that individual believers don't have to have a priest to get to God, and that churches don't have to have another ecclesiastical authority above them to run themselves. But at the same time, the Bible also teaches quite clearly that Christ has designed his churches to operate under the guidance and leadership of "pastor/teachers" (Eph. 4:11), also called "elders" in the New Testament. "Elder" was a term that carried with it a clear and definite sense of authority.

Let no reader jump to the conclusion that this book recommends a system of elder governance in the way that most people understand the term in the twenty-first century. To the contrary, we have a need to reinvestigate the biblical meaning of the term "elder," to see if it holds any vital implications for the way we conduct the life and business of churches in our day. It turns out that an honest evaluation of the New Testament material reveals that elders were not a board of directors that existed in addition to the pastors of the church, and that they were most definitely not synonymous with deacons.

In fact, an overview of references to elders in the New Testament will show that elders *were* the pastors of the churches, and that as such they did wisely and firmly exercise loving authority in the churches:

- Barnabas and Paul ordained elders to take charge of the newly planted churches where they took the gospel (Acts 14:3).
- The church at Antioch sent a delegation to Jerusalem to consult with Peter and the other apostles and elders about a dispute over circumcision. Clearly, the Antioch church intended to submit itself to the judgment (i.e. spiritual authority) of the larger body of elders.
- The Jerusalem elders, convinced by Peter of what the Holy Spirit was saying, arrived at a decision. By some

fashion they led the entire church to "sign on" to this decision—to agree—whereupon they sent a delegation back to Antioch to deliver the decision. The Antioch church, in turn, was prepared to accept what the elders had determined (Acts 15:22-23).
- After the Antioch church had adopted the guidelines laid out by the Jerusalem elders as their own, Paul and Silas toured cities where believers were, and imparted the elders' "decrees" concerning the circumcision matter (and perhaps others). Without question, these were directives, not suggestions (Acts 16:4).
- In Paul's goodbye address to the Ephesian elders, he made a point of saying they had been made "overseers" of the church (Acts 20:28). This passage, not accidentally, uses three terms referring to the same persons in the church: verse 28 is addressed to "elders," πρεσβυτερους (*presbuterous*) in the Greek; the verse then exhorts these elders to "feed" the "flock" ("feed" is ποιμαινειν (*poimainein*) and "flock" is ποιμνιο (*poimnio*), forms of the same word from which "pastor" (*poimenas*) also comes); and finally Paul states that these elders have been made "overseers" (*episkopous*) of the church. This passage clearly teaches, then, that the role of the pastor is also as elder and overseer. Elders are not some group of persons apart from the pastor(s) of the church. Elders or overseers *are* pastors, and vice versa. They are pastors in their role as decision makers and leaders with genuine, spiritual authority.

Not only in Acts, but in the rest of the New Testament, writers clearly indicate that elders/pastors/overseers filled roles of authority in the churches:

- Paul spoke of "elders that rule well" (1 Tim. 5:17), particularly those whose ministry was "in the word and doctrine (teaching)."
- Peter used the same three words—*presbuterous, poimanate,* and *episkopountes,* to refer to pastors in 1 Pet. 5:1-2, establishing again that pastors function in the roles of decision-making and oversight.

The bottom line of the matter is that the pastors of New Testament churches were God's gift to those churches to be leaders and decision makers, and he expected both that they would "have the rule" and that the congregations would show them "double honor" (1 Tim. 5:17) as such. Lest the casual reader of the Bible think this honor of which Paul speaks is merely a comfortable salary, recall the crystal clear instruction from Hebrews 13:17: "submit to their authority."

The vehement objection some church members have to the idea that their pastors should be accorded authority in the church is truly startling. Mention authority, or spiritual authority, and suddenly accusations fly of "dictatorship." Critics raise the specter of horrible abuses of power, and cite the political maxim, "Power corrupts," to support their view that pastors should be kept clear of any real sense of authority.

The irony of this position is that many churches are careful to make certain their pastors are not corrupted by having authority; but apparently they are not concerned about their own corruption from wielding all the authority themselves, or by delegating the task of running the church to deacons, which is even worse. The truth is that congregations are just as corruptible, and perhaps more so, because they comprise not only mature believers but many grossly immature ones as well.

If "power corrupts" were a biblical truth, no system of governance would be acceptable, since someone has to have authority, even if it is shared. But God's word does not make such a statement. In the real world, where every institution functions under some system of authority, God has placed in the church persons he intended to have the greater part of that authority, and those persons are the elders-pastors-overseers—what we call simply "pastors" today.

To the extent that pastors-in-training have not been taught the full dimension of their biblical role, they have gone into pastoral leadership under-prepared both to exercise the biblical leadership they were meant to have and to continue to educate churches about God's design. Consequently, after several generations of church members have fed on the idea that they or the deacons should run the church and that pastors serve at the deacons' or the churches' fickle discretion, pastors themselves occupy highly tenuous positions. They are constantly appeasing this or that group, playing politics with their "leadership decisions" (such as they are), and compromising their more challenging goals, simply because their survival demands it.

Many pastors lack any real power to do *anything* in their churches, beyond speaking publicly and pushing paper around a church office. The typical pastor is stymied by a complex system of internal politics, the lesser part of it in some form of constitution or bylaws but the greater part unwritten. Many pastors set out in their first churches to guide by the strength of their vision, only to learn that it is practically impossible to accomplish anything without learning how to subtly massage the political process at dozens of pressure points. Even then, especially after the honeymoon is over, they are likely to see general cooperation in only a few things, and overwhelming cooperation in almost none. Obviously, there are exceptional churches where this bleak view is foreign, and others where things aren't even *this* good.

Where, in the biblical model of shepherd and sheep, is there anything to suggest that this highly politicized version of church operation is anything like what the Lord meant to take place among his flock? Who will defend such a situation on even the remotest of biblical grounds?

## Promise them Anything

All this disrespect of the pastor in his role is carried out against the backdrop of church-wide claims of the opposite. How many pastors could tell of how pulpit committees and then perhaps deacons have told them—when they were merely candidates for the pastoral position—"We are a church full of opportunity for growth. All we need is a someone who will lead us, and we will go on to great things"—or some such boast. So he accepts the call, casts the vision, gets out in front and projects the goal, and suddenly he encounters one brick wall after another. It turns out that people don't want change. Yet, progress always involves change. In fact, the church members don't want to be led anywhere.

To be fair to many of these churches and their pulpit committees, it is not their intention to deceive. They simply want to put their best foot forward, show their best side, maximize their best qualities. Their sin is in both the degree to which they exaggerate their excellence, and also in their failure to recommit themselves to the ideals they project themselves as believing.

They were excited by the idea that they might be forward-looking people. They envisioned themselves developing and changing. But they did not adopt their own vision, or commit themselves to a forward look. When it came down to following the leader they called, they chose to replace him rather than follow him and change. They needed a pastor, and in their eagerness to fill their need they sold themselves as ready, willing, and able. They made whatever promises it took to entreat their chosen prospect.

Fundamentally, what is at work here besides people's natural dislike of change is a disrespect for pastoral leadership. A pastor is not merely a PTA president, elected for a term mostly because he is willing and nobody else wants the job. Quite to the contrary, pastors are God-called persons with a vision and a passion for what they do, and churches are supposed to be bodies of God-transformed individuals who have accepted the great commission of Christ and want to go forward in his name as a family of believers to accomplish something for God's glory. They should have a heightened sense of mission, and they should expect to hear in the word of their pastors the strains of the word of God.

## *Case Study 1*

The ABC Church in a Southeastern state elected a pulpit committee to find a replacement after a long pastorate. The committee elected three powerful persons, two men and a woman, and two "drones," both women who were pliable and basically unaware of the internal politics of the church. After a brief search, they came up with a candidate who matched their profile, which was unremarkable in its expectation of normal pastoral care and competent preaching. What stood out in the profile was their statement of desire for a true leader, someone who could take a difficult situation of decline and help their church grow again. In turn, they pledged to follow and work.

Upon a vote indicating an acceptable majority of about 90%, the candidate accepted their call to be pastor. But within two months, the church had reneged on its promise.

The pastor attempted to lead deacons in a membership recovery plan; but all but two of them did not follow through with any contacts or assignments the pastor gave them.

Seeing the continuing decline and sensing conflict approaching, the church's minister of music quickly found another place of service. Within three months the church called a full time minister of music. He and the pastor were the only ministerial staff members. They became very good friends, and shared both a vision for reaching the immediate community and for leading the church in the spirit of the New Testament pastors and elders.

However, the church's failure to commit itself honestly to change was coming to quick fruition. What the pulpit committee had initially expressed as a desire for a true leader, who would help them achieve their desire to grow, more honestly should have been stated: we want someone to turn the church around on a dime and make us what we used to be. Under complex circumstances (as they always are), the pastor could not fulfill their desires. The internal powers held informal and secret meetings, and promptly laid out before the pastor their insistence that he leave, so they could find a leader who would take them where they wanted to go. Seeing he could not win, even if he won, the pastor resigned.

Here was a church whose internal leadership did not respect the position and the calling of the pastor. Since they did not accord the pastor the true authority to lead, they disrespected him as their elder. Their argument might have been that they did not believe he was being led of God—else certainly they would have followed. But more likely they rejected his leadership by God because they didn't like the emphasis of his ministry and the change and commitment it required of them.

## Case Study 2

The EFG Church of a Midwestern city became embroiled in a denominational dispute precipitated by division over a nearby affiliated college weaning itself away from the parent body. The pastor, a supporter of the college, fell out of favor with about half the congregation, and found another place of service before the situation grew unbearable. Amid declining membership, the church called a pastor they believed would be tolerant to both sides in the dispute. However, supporters of the college in the church increased, and eventually dominated its internal theological politics.

This group, which was characterized not only by its support of the college but its theological viewpoint on related issues, saw the pastor as on an opposing side, simply because he declined to make support of the college an issue. The pastor, for his part, believed that his role in the church was not to support a college, but to preach the gospel, teach and make disciples, and lead the church to reach people for Christ. His sense of direction for the church was undergirded by the fact that the town had entered a period of transition in which traditional sources of membership were drying up, and the church was facing the necessity of renewing its dream, or else dying. The church's position on the nearby college was of little value in its recovery from decline.

Unfortunately for the pastor, the internal powers that had always ruled the church—the ever-growing body of deacons, present and past—did not share his conviction. Among quite a few prominent couples in the church, at least one worked in some capacity at the college, and thus the entrenched leadership did not see support of the college as a "non issue." The wheels of disgruntlement began to turn. Wearied by resistance and unable to accomplish anything in the highly charged atmosphere, the pastor sensed the imminence of enmity. He called on his network of friends, and turned up several opportunities, one of which he promptly took.

What happened afterward demonstrated the church's fundamental disrespect for the pastor's authority in leadership of the church. College supporters skillfully manipulated the selection of a pastor search committee, which duly recommended to the church a pastor who, while willing to go on record supporting the local college, was also duly willing to say anything else the internal leadership wanted, and to craft his plan of ministry according to the strong, preconceived interests of those same leaders. Unfortunately, since they did not have a vision for the church's challenge in the community, and had a pastor who simply mirrored their thinking, the church continued to stagnate, and has not recovered.

## Perilous Rejection

A church's disrespect for its pastor's (or its pastors') authority in leadership is impractical at the least; but at its worst it is a perilous rejection not only of the pastor's leadership, but also of the Lord's. Since the Lord Jesus Christ by his Spirit "gave some apostles, some prophets, some evangelists, and some pastor/ teachers" to the church, a church is disrespecting the design and intention of Christ in refusing to accept the authoritative mission of the pastor.

When Jesus sent out the seventy disciples on a preaching and healing tour, he told them that people who received them received him, and vice versa: those who rejected them rejected him. Further, he added that those who rejected him rejected the Father who sent him (Luke 10:16). The principle he taught was that people cannot free themselves from accountability to God by suggesting that he "not take it personally." Any rejection of God's plan mediated through his representatives—be they pastors, evangelists, parents, or a providentially appointed stranger—is a rejection of God. This principle of powers being ordained by God is what makes the church's disrespect of its pastor's mission and authority such a perilous thing. A reasonable consideration of the probable response of Christ must conclude that a church rejecting his appointed authority invites his discipline.

The experience of Ezekiel with the Jews prefigured the conflict of many a church with those whom God sends to lead it. Meditating before the Lord, Ezekiel heard God say:

> **"Your countrymen are talking together about you by the walls and at the doors of the houses, saying to each other, 'Come and hear the message that has come from the Lord.' My people come to you, as they usually do, and sit before you to listen to your words, but they do not put them into practice."**
> **Ezekiel 33:31 NIV**

A sense of religious obligation, or a general belief in the concept of getting direction and blessing from God, prompted the Jews to listen to Ezekiel prophesy. As church members say today, they "went to preaching." But they did not implement what Ezekiel said. They showed surface respect by attendance, but they demonstrated underlying and ultimate disrespect of Ezekiel's ministry by chronically choosing to dismiss what he said, doing as they liked instead.

Is there a more fitting description of the rebellious character of many churches today? They dutifully call pastors—because that's what churches do, after all; but then they ignore much of the passionate teaching and preaching of those pastors, and insist on ruling their own roosts, in defiance of God's plan to lead them through their pastors' vision. Many if not most churches with some sort of congregational government by definition do not vest the head pastor, or the staff in general, with any significant level of authority to make decisions on behalf of the church. But in many of those churches, even when there is tacit acknowledgment of the pastor's spiritual authority, the church functions as if he were there only to conduct inspiring "worship experiences." Many such churches want the preacher to leave the decision making to them.

## Case Study 3

The JKL Church of a languid rural community in the Midwest had roots going back before the Civil War. They had called numerous pastors in their history, most of whom were young. Their proximity to a seminary made finding prospective ministers easy, and many a seminarian had spent the last year of his schooling plus two or three additional years laboring in JKL's field.

JKL's newest pastor was a capable preacher, which delighted the congregation. He was also a young man with ideas, which he attempted to introduce in the church's life. During his first few months at the church, he learned that the deacons determined the business of the church, and he determined to bring up ideas for change in their meetings.

The deacons met Sunday nights after church once a month. In his first meeting with them, the young pastor hoped to have a chance to speak. The chairman conducted the meeting with no reference to the pastor at all, until the end, at which time he called on the pastor "for a word." When the young minister began to lay out some of his plans, the chairman spoke up, telling him that they would need to discuss his plans in private and bring them up at a later date.

In subsequent meetings, the chairman either did not call on the pastor at all, or did so at the end of the meeting, specifying that he was recognizing the pastor to give a "devotional word." Finally, after the pastor attempted in one more meeting to introduce his ideas for organizational change, the deacon chairman visited him in his office the next day to say, "Pastor, we want you to preach, visit the sick, and win the lost. Leave the business of the church to us."

Many a young and green minister has been employed by a church looking for someone to perform required services, but has not been allowed to begin to implement any of the vision God may have given to him. While these churches probably have not written into their constitutional documents any specific language limiting the pastor's role to those services that could be defined as "spiritual maintenance," in practice this is what they expect. They prefer that their pastors leave the business of the church to them. After all, they regard pastors as transitional and temporary, while they, the members, are permanent. Since they aren't going anywhere, and will live with the results of changes instituted by pastors, they prefer to keep such changes to a bare minimum.

This stifling of the leadership desire God gives ministers is the outworking of the fundamental disrespect many churches have for the person the New Testament calls an "elder:" the pastor or pastors of the church. It represents a reversal of the concept of leadership God designed into the church as reflected in the New Testament. And its destructive effect is not limited to the particular church where it is the prevailing philosophy. Many churches, having a ready supply of young ministers going through them every few years, manage to condition these young men to be timid instead of aggressive, and to "learn their place" instead of developing their vision. So gelded, young pastors may go from place to place becoming more docile in each, never realizing the dreams God gave them.

That this lost vision is ultimately the minister's responsibility is undeniable. But that churches disrespecting the pastor's mission are culpable as well is equally undeniable.

Churches that do not respect the authority and leadership of the pastors or elders God has sent them demonstrate a usurpation of authority. But they are not eager to bear the responsibility for the outcome. For one of the subtle ways in which churches defeat their pastors and destroy themselves is by maintaining a double standard, as we shall see.

# 3

# The Double Standard

**Preach the word; be instant in season, out of season; reprove, rebuke, exhort with all longsuffering and doctrine.**
**2 Timothy 4:2**

**...And at that time there was a great persecution against the church which was at Jerusalem; and they were all scattered abroad throughout the regions of Judaea and Samaria, except the apostles. ...Therefore they that were scattered abroad went every where preaching the word.**
**Acts 8:1,4**

Every pastor has experienced the double standard applied to clergy or laity, minister or member, parson or people. The simple fact is that church members have expectations of pastors *as people* that they would never accept for themselves.

This double standard displays itself in numerous ways, some of which have become an expected part of pastoral territory:

- The average person in the pew expects his pastor to be a much better Christian than he, not just in the matter of how much he knows, but in general spirituality, moral stature, and ethical performance as well. The typical layman will deny that he thinks he can be justifiably less moral or ethical than the preacher, but on a deeper, perhaps subliminal level, he assumes he can.
- The pastor is expected not to have any bad habits, particularly smoking and drinking. Yet every church has its "outstanding men," those who can be found standing outside smoking between Sunday School and church, and almost no one thinks it justified to label this activity "wrong"—politically incorrect, yes; unhealthy, yes; but not wrong, as it would be for the pastor to do it. And in every congregation, even the most conservative of Baptist congregations, there are those who imbibe various levels of intoxicants with impunity.
- Pastors are not permitted to have very close friends within the church membership, lest they play favorites in any way. However, church members at large not only defend the principle that they should have close friends and cannot be close to everyone, but they carry their freedom of association to the level of establishing tight cliques. These cliques are responsible for warding off potential members right and left, as any preacher who has gone to see offended visitors knows.
- The pastor's wife is expected to be the co-pastor, the

most gracious hostess in the church, a woman's missionary society leader, and to sing in the choir, lead a children's choir, and anything else the church can think up, or that the previous pastor's wife did. However, no other woman in the church is expected to hold any position or render any service simply because her husband holds a particular office.
- A pastor's children are expected to be better than any other children. They may be told so by Sunday School teachers, and if they misbehave, a deacon will take it upon himself to inform the pastor in the gravest of manners.

More examples exist. These instances of the application of a double standard are, however, of *relatively* minor importance.

In the case of those double standards where personal habits are involved, depending on the severity of the issue pastors have sometimes simply conceded their inability to effect change.

In the case of double standards involving traditions, most pastors have developed ways to deal with the pesky inequities to which they become heir when they accept a call to ministry. Some ignore the unfair expectations and take the heat until it subsides. Some confront such issues in one way or another and dare anyone to defend the indefensible. But a pastor's—or his family's—refusal to play the double standard game rarely causes serious trouble by itself, apart from some deeper issue.

The really crucial issue involving a double standard exists at a deeper level and involves consequences more costly to the church and the pastor or staff. This is the double standard of responsibility. Simply stated:

***Many church members hold the pastor responsible for the success of the church; but they are not willing to shoulder their share of the responsibility.***

The scriptures quoted at the top of this chapter may have seemed unrelated to the chapter title, but they are not. Here is the connection:

- The passage from 2 Timothy is Paul's familiar instruction to Timothy, *a pastor,* to "preach the word." Virtually every Christian knows this verse applies to all pastors: they are to know and proclaim the Bible.
- The passage from Acts describes how, upon being persecuted greatly for the first time, the church at Jerusalem was scattered to regions all around Judea and beyond. The apostles, however, stayed in Jerusalem. The apostles were the pastors of that first church. So, get the picture clearly: the *church members* scattered, and the *pastors* stayed. And who does Acts say began preaching the word of God everywhere? *The church members.*

There it is: Pastors are to proclaim the word and the gospel, and so are church members. Pastors are to witness, and so are church members. Pastors are to do outreach, but so are church members. In fact, if church members in general are not involved in witness and outreach, a church will dwindle and die eventually. Neither is it solely the pastor's duty to witness and win the lost, nor is it possible for him to perform this task sufficiently on the church field. Yet the typical pastor is held to a standard that makes him responsible for these duties, and for the ultimate success of the church in terms of growth, while church members do not generally hold themselves responsible for the same thing.

## The Half Truth

The pastor who has wrangled with this double standard of responsibility may indeed have tried to communicate to his flock that they are expected to engage in outreach and witnessing.

Something of a recovery of truth has taken place concerning the scripture's teaching about ministry. In the past generation or so, seminaries have stressed to their students that Paul's statements in Ephesians 4:11 make clear that apostles, prophets, evangelists, and pastor-teachers are to equip the saints, and the saints—*church members*—are to go do the work of ministry (along with the pastor, of course). A typical reading of that verse throughout history has it backwards, suggesting that pastors and other ministers are to do all the work of the ministry. Pastors have learned their true role is to be equippers of the saints. But as pastors have gone out into the churches and tried to tell the saints this wonderful revelation, they have encountered the strongest resistance. It is still quite common to hear folks in the pew say, "We pay the preacher to do that."

What makes it so difficult for pastors to retrain congregations to understand their own responsibility for "preaching the word" (Acts 8:4) is the fact that the pastor as a leader has an extra measure of this responsibility. Congregations that hold the pastor, but not themselves, responsible for the success of the church are not entirely wrong in making him accountable. He is accountable for the church's outreach; and because he is a leader, he is somewhat more accountable than the average church member—not necessarily to *do* more outreach personally than anyone, but to *lead* the church in outreach and witnessing.

Consequently, the double standard of responsibility is based on a half truth: that pastors are more responsible than church members for the success of the church. But they are not mostly or entirely responsible, which is what many church members assume. The double standard exists in the degree to which church members hold the pastor responsible for the church's growth and prosperity.

Drawing the line that defines just how responsible a pastor is would be difficult, and probably is unnecessary for this discussion. The general truth is readily provable, as any pastor could testify.

And the result of this double standard is that many pastors "get the boot" because of the church's lack of success. Here's the way it goes:

The pastor has "failed" to take the church to the heights of glory that someone or ones assumed he should have. Perhaps he has simply failed to pull a dying church out of the doldrums. Maybe he has been unsuccessful in keeping a neighboring church (usually a strong, regional congregation) from stealing members in an ever-increasing stream. As decline or stagnation sets in, church members who indulge in comparing the church to others in the area, or to some church on television, or to what their own church used to be like, become dissatisfied and frustrated. Their attention turns first, and automatically, to the pastor. It must be his fault. They assume he hasn't visited enough, or hasn't won enough people to Christ, or hasn't followed up on all the visitors. Some church members give lip service to the concept of their own involvement in outreach, but they claim the pastor hasn't led them sufficiently in that endeavor. They may conveniently forget the sermons or Bible studies he has conducted on witnessing, or the visitations he has organized and which they have not attended. No, he hasn't done his job, and because of that sad fact, they are failing.

Conscientious pastors often have a wide streak of guilt running through them, and frequently face such crises by telling themselves that they have, indeed, failed. They haven't witnessed enough, or led strongly enough. They have "left their first love" (Rev. 2:4). In fact, there may be some truth to these soul-searching conclusions. But most of the time the pastor would be engaging in a false and self-destructive "humility" to accept all or most of the blame for what is happening in his church. Most of the time, the church membership bears a large share of the responsibility, but it is not acknowledging or accepting that responsibility.

The half truth behind the double standard of responsibility, namely that the pastor is somewhat more responsible for the church's success than other church members, is blown into "the whole truth" by typical churches whenever trouble brews. The reason for this exaggeration of the pastor's culpability is obvious: church members cannot justify terminating the pastor or forcing him to resign if the grounds are not sufficient. If he has not been caught in immorality, if he has not played golf every day instead of going to the office, if he has not preached or taught things that are theologically embarrassing or unacceptable to the congregation, then he must be stuck with the entire blame for the church's lack of growth and success. Even though those who insist on his replacement may not be able to put their finger on any particular failure, or explain just how the pastor has failed, to their minds it is the only conclusion left to the reasonable person: the church isn't going anywhere, so the pastor must not be doing his job.

The other reason church members enlarge the half truth into the whole truth, which is really the great lie, and make the pastor solely responsible for the church's failure, is that they are unwilling to accept any blame themselves. To do so would be to imply that:

- They must confess their sins and repent of their lack of obedience to the great commission;
- They must surrender their own lives afresh to the Lordship of Christ and the mastery of the Holy Spirit;
- They must seek renewal and revival for the entire church;
- They must accept the possibility that the church may not discover or recover prosperity overnight;
- They must commit themselves to being faithful in outreach and witnessing until the church does begin to grow and prosper, and then continue that lifestyle;
- They must forego any inclination they may have had to pressure the pastor to resign, and must begin to pray for him instead, as they do their part;
- They must learn a new way of looking at the church's "success," refusing to compare their church unreasonably to other churches whose circumstances may be entirely different.

There may be other things church members would have to do if they accepted the notion that they were responsible for their church's languishing life; but this list alone—unconsciously perceived—is enough to send the typical Christian looking for some scapegoat to pin the church's problems on.

## Case Study 4

In a burgeoning city of one of the eastern states, the MNO Church had existed in an old neighborhood for nearly fifty years. At times in their past, they had boasted a membership of nearly five hundred. As the city grew larger, however, their neighborhood took on more and more characteristics of the inner-city. It became less cohesive and homogeneous. Drug use went up, and many dwellings were occupied by unmarried couples and homosexuals. Older Christian couples died off or moved away, and younger Christian couples simply avoided the neighborhood. The church began to decline.

Their beloved pastor of long years was called—loudly—to another field. So MNO sought and found another pastor. During the interim they cheer-led themselves to believe that their team could and would win the battle against a declining neighborhood, and would again prosper and grow. When the new pastor arrived, they breathed a sigh of relief that a new day had dawned. A layman who had risen to the challenge of pulling the church through its interim crisis promptly resigned all his posts and announced to the new pastor, privately of course, that he was exhausted. Another member family, who had been decreasingly involved for several years but had joined the frenzy of self-induced enthusiasm about the church's prophesied recovery, told the pastor, also in private, that they had decided to give the church "another try." Several other members shared the same "wait-and-see" attitude. Essentially, dozens of members had decided to give the new pastor a few months to make the church successful again, after which, if he didn't, either they would leave, or he would.

The new pastor assessed the situation and concluded that the church was not going to become a regional congregation because of its location, and that it was not going to appeal widely to persons in outlying, more prosperous neighborhoods. Instead, it was going to have to reach the down-and-outs, drop-outs, and doped-outs, and the divorced, diseased, decrepit, derelict and detoxified denizens in its own neighborhood. The pastor succeeded in convincing very few people to join him in this quest, but he forged ahead nonetheless. After a few additions to the church from this group of prospects—who after all increasingly made up the neighborhood—the powers that be in the church began to complain. This is not the kind of success they had envisioned.

The next chapter of the story is predictable. Since the pastor had not succeeded in getting back the members who had drifted away (who were mostly attending nearby, successful churches), and since he had not succeeded in reaching affluent communities lying outside the church's immediate neighborhood, he had failed in his responsibility. And since some of those who had stuck around to see what happened were definitely not of the same socio-economic strata as the persons now coming into the church, they were not interested in prolonging the "opportunity" they had given the new pastor to keep them. They quickly dropped off like bees from a sprayed hive, and cited the pastor's failure as their reason.

The powers that be, who were deeply entrenched in the church and were not willing to leave it, turned up the heat on the pastor, eventually forcing him to resign or be party to splitting the church. They promptly found a new pastor, convincing him that the only reason for their dismal statistics was the previous pastor's failure to perform. The new pastor instituted a growth campaign following traditional methods; but in two years the statistics of the church were just as dismal, and even worse.

Still, the widely held belief of church members was that it was the fault of their previous pastors, soon to be joined by their present one, that the church had not "succeeded," however they measured success. Scarcely any of them every invited prospects to church, or witnessed or won anyone to Christ. Hardly any of them could be begged, threatened or cajoled into sharing in the follow-up of visitors. And few of them wanted new members from the neighborhood immediately surrounding them. Yet they were unwilling to accept responsibility for their church's failure to grow and succeed. All of that responsibility they placed on a string of pastors.

With few changes to the details, the previous case study would describe the experience of thousands of churches and pastors. Two sides usually exist to any story, and in fact the stories many of us hear resemble the church-member version, since potential raconteurs of their version outnumber pastors a hundred to one. But in this day of epidemic forced terminations of pastors, when few of the incidents are precipitated by immorality or gross negligence, is it reasonable to believe the simplistic accusation that pastors are unilaterally to blame? Hardly.

And this is precisely the premise of this chapter: that many churches apply a double standard of responsibility to themselves and their pastors. They make pastors almost entirely to blame for their failure to grow, accepting virtually none of the responsibility themselves. Even on the face of it, this lopsided blame is improbable, and it becomes recognizable for the lie that it is when the evidence is inspected.

## Firing the Coach

Since the double standard holds the pastor responsible for the church's failure to grow, the remedy usually applied affects him primarily: he is voted or pressured out. Since the church members who forced him to leave do not accept any responsibility themselves, they stay.

The situation is somewhat analogous to sports teams. It is proverbial that when a team loses, they fire the coach. In the proverb, "loses" means "continually loses, and "they" means the owners. Sometimes the coach genuinely bears some or most of the responsibility. Often, however, he never had a chance, for one reason or another.

After the 2002 Major League Baseball season, five managers of major league teams were promptly fired. Among them was Bobby Valentine of the New York Mets.

Two years before, Valentine had led the team to a World Series Championship. But in 2002, the team finished last in its division. Was the team's 2002 failure Bobby's fault? If the answer is yes, then was the team's 2000 championship creditable mostly to Bobby? If so, then why, and how, did Bobby change so drastically in two years? Insiders know that Bobby didn't change much if at all. A talented but eccentric and complicated person, Bobby had his friends and his enemies, and was successful in motivating some players and not others. But he was not much different in 2002 from 2000. Obviously, more things were at work than Bobby Valentine's personal performance. The team itself changed drastically, with the departure of numerous players.

Or consider the case of the Florida Marlins. Before the 1997 season, Marlins owners pulled out all the financial stops to buy themselves a team that could win the World Series. In 1997, they hired Jim Leyland as manager, and the team won the Series that season. The following year, the Marlins began divesting themselves of the costliest players, having blown their wad the previous season. They finished with 54 wins and 108 losses, and Leyland quit, to save the Marlins the trouble of firing him for having a losing season. Whose fault was it—Leylands? Clearly not. He was sandbagged.

Sometimes the team is bad, and there is nothing the manager can do to fix things.

Sometimes in churches, the members, not the pastor, are to blame for the church's failure to grow and succeed. A church can fire or make life miserable for half a dozen pastors in a row, and essentially nothing will change, because the wrong people are leaving. The sad fact is, this very thing frequently happens. Some churches get a reputation for this kind of conduct, wearing without interruption the blinders of denial that they bear tremendous responsibility themselves for their church's success. Sometimes it's the manager who needs to fire the team—but that's not how things work.

At least, it isn't how things work anymore. Several generations have passed since church discipline of members was common, but it still exists in the cultural memory. Not just for immorality but sometimes for gross negligence of general Christian duty, members could be censured or even put out of the church by the rest of the body. And many church bodies, led by committed pastors, often did police themselves in this way.

Some church constitutions or covenants still provide for such remedies for a church member's irresponsibility. But few churches hold themselves accountable anymore for their corporate responsibility for their own success and growth. Those that do discover the blessing of God's revival fire. Those that don't, plane out, atrophy, and/or die. As one pastor put it, "My church members don't think we need to plant new churches because we have so many already; and we do, but we don't have many healthy ones. Most of them are dying."

Not only do many churches contribute to their own demise because they rest almost the entire weight of their success on their pastors, but in displacing their pastors, they sometimes contribute to those ministers' permanent defeat. An increasing number of pastors, treated shabbily by demanding congregations, enter a spiral of defeat that too often leads to their permanent exodus from career ministry. Their families are hurt financially, and potentially in many other ways. Not just a few children of dismissed pastors have developed their own bitterness about the way Dad was treated, and have become less involved in varying degrees in church life themselves.

The double standard church members apply to themselves and their pastors is one factor assisting those churches in suicide. A church that hangs its success primarily on the talent, energy, devotion and charisma of its pastor is a church that is headed for dusty death.

Church members' disavowal of their own responsibility for growth and success is a nail in their church's coffin. Closely related to this abandonment of duty is the extra burden of expectation churches place on their pastors. As we shall see, expecting too much of a pastor helps defeat him as he struggles to perform, and helps destroy the church.

# 4

# Expecting Too Much

**To the weak became I as weak, that I might gain the weak: I am made all things to all men, that I might by all means save some.**
**1 Corinthians 9:22**

**And Moses' father in law said unto him, The thing that thou doest is not good. Thou wilt surely wear away, both thou, and this people that is with thee: for this thing is too heavy for thee; thou art not able to perform it thyself alone.**
**Exodus 18:17-18**

When Paul told the Corinthian church he had become "all things to all men," he didn't have in mind attempting to perform expertly every ministry in the church by himself. He meant he attempted to adapt to every situation, to relate to everyone as best he could, so as to be able to communicate the gospel. Unfortunately, his pronouncement in 1 Cor. 9:22 could be the motto of many churches as to their expectations of their pastors: 'We want a man who can do it all, and ring everybody's chimes; and by all means, we want him to win the community to Christ.'

Faced with such expectations, many pastors try valiantly to meet them. But like the chameleon who one day walked across a piece of Scotch plaid and died valiantly trying to adjust, the pastor who attempts the same eventually fails.

The truth about the pastor's inability to be everything to everyone was uttered in simple words by Moses' father in law: 'You try to do it all yourself and you'll wear out, and you'll take these people down with you.' Jethro was speaking of the sheer load of the one job of Moses' judicial work; but the principle holds true of trying to do too many jobs. Pastors by and large have attempted to manage their time so that they have some hours free in the day, get days off in the week, and get weeks off in the year. Some even manage to convince their churches to give them a sabbatical every so many years.

But some of these same pastors, under the constant pressure of their churches to perform with increasing proficiency in many areas of church work, bend to the pressure by trying to stuff more and more into the somewhat reasonable hours they do work. The result, all too often, is that they either wind up having to take shortcuts in some or all of these duties, or they become clinically depressed and may snap under the stress.

Why do many churches expect too much of their pastors? It is reasonable to assume that it is not intentional. But the fact that church members do not set out to lay too much burden on one person in leadership does not mean that the underlying reasons are not deliberate. The contributing causes to the extremely high expectation frequently held by churches are fairly simple.

*The typical pastor's excessive workload is not the result of an incidental lack of foresight or the happy byproduct of the blessings of church growth. It is the consequence of defective ideas about pastoral ministry and deficient member stewardship.*

## The Evolution of the Pastorate

One reason churches in general have come to expect too much of their pastors is that the concept of the pastor's role has evolved slowly in the direction of multifaceted ministry. In the Western world in particular, the church has slowly adapted to the market principles at work in the general culture. People "shop" for churches, comparing the features of one church to another. Pastors increasingly have recognized this trend, and have attempted to institute great variety in existing ministries, and to add other ministries and features to their churches, in an attempt to attract people:

- As the sophistication of organizations in the church has increased, so has the demand for more intricate and involved administration of these organizations.

Frequently, pastors report that the role in which they find the most demanding expectations, but for which they have the least effective ability, is that of administration.

When a church has no minister of education or his equivalent, usually the pastor is expected to keep the Sunday School organized and properly motivated—even when the Sunday School may have a director. Discipleship programs, prayer programs, benevolence programs, seniors programs, youth programs, even music programs, may wind up being administered by the lone pastor in churches where no other ministers labor.

When churches do acquire additional ministers and/or support staff, the pastor, wearing his administration hat, must spend time supervising, giving guidance, counseling, working out problems between staff members, and both communicating and constantly reemphasizing or explaining his vision. While many solo pastors have dreamt of having other staff members to share the load, the fact is that more staff means more administration, which tends to balance out the equation.

- Nor is it enough to be a simple but competent preacher these days. In earlier times, people heard far fewer preachers with whom to compare their own; but today, with transportation what it is, people easily travel even to other cities to go to church and hear Pastor Greatness in First Church, Big Town. And with the media being what it is, church members can turn on the radio or television and hear or see the dynamic Dr. Wonderful, whose ministry changes thousands and spans the globe, or better. Far too many of these enchanted church members find a way to mention to their pastors that they heard Dr. Wonderful say such and such, or that they saw Pastor Great do this or that, and then they leave the conclusion to the pastor: "I wish you would do it this way"—or even, "If you can't match what I get elsewhere, I'll *go* elsewhere." Unfortunately, the solution often is even worse: "If you can't compete, *you'll* go elsewhere."

As a result, the pastor is forced (or thinks he is) to develop a more "dynamic" style, or to add a degree to his name, or to buy more books and use some of the competition's outlines, or to watch Dr. Wonderful and adopt his mannerisms, or to spice up his presentations with the same kind of stories or jokes. In the effort to become someone else, he stops being who he is, which may have been just what God wanted him to be.

- In Western culture in particular, churches have come to be seen as bearing the responsibility of offering some activity for every conceivable church group, and maintaining both the facilities for, and the organization for, all these activities. This expectation demands buildings, and pastors are expected to work closely with architects and contractors, as well as organizing and insuring the success of a fund-raising program to pay for the looming edifices. They are to be as effective in promoting these capital funds campaigns as experts

who have studied and carried out these special programs for years. If Rev. Pledgegetter on TV can raise a million dollars for his new mission to build a prayer cathedral, surely the local pastor can squeeze enough out of the good folks in his flock to pay for the family life building.
- Expectations are ever increasing for more specialized ministries and services on Sundays, as well as during the week. Today's pastor is often expected to prepare a children's sermon, managing a squirming cluster of preschoolers to grade-schoolers with the expertise and aplomb of a seasoned kindergarten teacher, while delivering weekly a fresh and innovative presentation of perfectly suited material to hold the children's attention and leave them with lasting, powerful lessons. Next Sunday, he will have to prepare and lead, in a dignified way, a dedication service for babies, a relatively new expectation of churches that do not baptize infants.
- The list of expectations of the pastor would continue *ad infinitum* by simply including the dizzying array of committee meetings, counseling appointments, rehearsals, and denominational seminars and sessions he is expected to attend, not to mention lunches, suppers and fellowships to which he is invited, whose hosts and hostesses he will offend if he does not go.

Any pastor can add one or two more expectations to this list. Taken alone, few if any in the list would be a problem; but taken all together, they compose a burdensome task of

Mosaic proportions.

Some preachers unwittingly compound their own problem of over-expectant members by attempting to "do it all." Some pastors are extraordinarily blessed with abilities, and begin many a ministry on the strength of their talents, and then find they have overextended themselves. Others, particularly in small churches, set a pattern early in their ministries of having their thumbs in every pie. As their churches grow, or as they move to larger places, the pies multiply, and they run out of fingers. Other pastors cheat their families and ultimately themselves of time and attention, and burn out while attempting to keep all other church fires adequately stoked. They don't listen to Jethro: "What you're doing is not good: you will wear yourself out."

Moses was fortunate to have a father-in-law who approached him about his over-burdensome workload. Every church needs lay leaders who have enough spiritual maturity about them to recognize when the church is placing too many demands upon its pastor. For sheer volume of the workload in the traditional ministries of the church—crisis ministry, benevolence, or meeting other family needs—the early church chose deacons. These persons were to be servants of the church under the direction of the elders, the apostles. In most churches today, however, deacons have shunned the role of obscure service for the more prestigious role of board members, leaving pastors again to bear most of the burden of ministry to families and individuals. When, because of church size and the neediness of church members, this individual attention eats into the pastor's time to prepare to preach or teach, or to handle the dozens of other things he is expected to do, the deacons may be the first to express their concern about his neglect, when it was they who should have been relieving some of this burden in the first place.

Unfortunately for the pastor, it is not enough to train the deacons to perform some of this ministry that they should have been doing. It is not enough because quite widely church members have developed the expectation that the pastor, not *a* pastor or another minister, not deacons, not Sunday School teachers or anyone else, but that *the* pastor should meet their needs, whatever they are, and that no one else will do. While this may be reasonable in a congregation of a hundred, it begins to decrease in reasonableness as the membership of the church increases, and at some point it becomes altogether impossible. Exactly where that line of reasonableness is differs for churches and pastors, but the line exists everywhere, and is routinely ignored by many church members.

Almost every pastor has trembled with joy at hearing some member say, "Pastor, I don't want you to feel that you need to come visit me unless I am at death's door and I call you. You have too much else to do." But for every one of those, there are fifty others who will never say to his face, but who may say behind his back, that they expect him to tread the neighborhood streets constantly, to see their relatives in the nursing homes once a month, to come by their hospital rooms every day, to call them when they have the flu, and to anticipate and meet many other miscellaneous needs. In fact, in churches of two hundred or more people it is not uncommon to hear some people say that they were absent from church for two weeks and the pastor didn't notice, and didn't call to see why, and didn't come by to see if there were something he could do. Many pastors do well just to read all the announcements they are handed ten minutes before the service, and to see their notes and concentrate on their sermons, without having to be expected to notice who is and is not present in worship. But it's just one more expectation church members feel no hesitation about piling on the pastor.

### The Need for Multiple Staff

The pastor's role, through the process of gradual evolution, has moved in the direction of multifaceted ministry. However, as the demands of churches and consumer-worshipers have increased, churches have not kept pace with these demands by adding pastors.

The first church in Jerusalem started out with at least twelve pastors. Most of the other churches mentioned in the New Testament evidently had more than one pastor, even from their inceptions. Paul opened his letter to the Philippian church with a greeting to the "bishops [pastors] and deacons." How many pastors the church at Philippi had, we do not know, but we may surmise they had enough to handle the load of ministry in the church.

Paul specifically told Titus to "ordain elders in every

city," an instruction to provide the congregations in the cities of Crete with several elders each. It is worth noting that Paul put Titus in charge of this selection of elders—a phenomenon today's Christians should study more deeply as we ponder the way the New Testament churches operated.

In Paul's first letter to Timothy, he refers to multiple elders, who administer the affairs of the church ("rule well"), some of whom (but not all, apparently) were preachers and teachers (1 Tim. 5:17). Taken together, the references in Paul's letters and Luke's account in Acts paint a picture of churches with multiple elders who had a division of labor to accomplish the various facets of ministry in the early church.

Why, then, do most churches today operate on the assumption that the normal condition of a church is to have only one pastor? Even many large churches have only one, though some have acquired associate or assistant pastors, and fewer still have executive pastors, who are usually administrators. Would not more churches profit by having multiple pastors to share the work of ministry?

Without doubt, they would. But churches resist acquiring additional pastors until the need is extreme, which usually means that there is extensive dissatisfaction with the lone pastor's performance. Occasionally, the solo pastor can convince his congregation to provide for the need before it becomes critical. But in typical churches of most denominations, the concept prevails that the church has only one pastor: any other persons are just helpers.

At root, this is a fundamental failure to properly interpret the New Testament. Even though Peter in Jerusalem, John (later) in Ephesus, and others, appear to have been accorded the role of "leading elder" in their respective churches, every indication is that the other elders in these congregations were thought of as elders or pastors in every respect.

Today, the closest thing most Protestant churches have to the New Testament model is other staff ministers laboring in music, youth, or education, or working especially with seniors, singles, or children, etc. While their churches may call them "Music Ministers," and so on, in fact they often correspond very closely to what various elders in the New Testament church were. An honest evaluation of the role of staff ministers in modern churches would suggest that often they should be more accurately referred to as "Pastor in Music, Pastor in Education, Pastor to Singles," etc. In some cases, they are. What needs to take place is a recovery of a biblical model in which multiple ministers labor together to meet the needs of congregations, specializing where necessary but sharing common roles as pastors to the body of saints. Denominations need to teach in their seminaries that ministers of all kinds are team members in the same work; and those ministers need to be trained in general pastoral work, so as to be able to minister to people along with the lead pastor. Finally, a whole generation of new Christians and church members needs to be taught to consider the ministry of any staff minister as equal to another if the need itself is met.

A revolution of the kind just described may never take place. The first requisite of such reformation would be the changed minds of a generation of ministers, and ironically, many ministers are not open to this new perspective. Some pastors are afraid of a diminished role, or may enjoy too much the heightened sense of importance resulting from their being the only pastor.

For the most part, however, the lack of additional pastors/elders/ministers to meet ministry needs can be attributed to the reluctance of church members to support the concept of multiple staff members—beyond the additional minister of music and/or youth that many churches add, some of whom are never more than part time.

## A Stewardship Problem

One reason for churches' reluctance to adopt the concept of multiple pastors is their typical inability to support such a staff. That inability, in turn, is due to churches' failure to be obedient in stewardship.

At budget preparation time, many a church has heard its pastor (or, more remarkably, some insightful layman) recite statistics suggesting that if even just the active members were to tithe, the church would have more money than it knew what to do with. For instance, in a church with only a hundred active families making an average of $50,000 per year (these day, almost a low figure most places), the church would receive $500,000 in gifts if all those families tithed. If all church members could be convinced to be good stewards, the same church, which might have two hundred families, could adopt a budget of a $1 million.

Usually, however, a church of that size might have a budget around $200,000, enabling them to support a pastor and a part time music "director," whom they don't even expect to have any pastoral functions. Yet the half or more families who don't give and aren't active usually have the same expectations of pastoral visits when they are sick, prayers when they are dying, and counsel when they are divorcing. If stewardship were what it should be, the church of 200 families should not only want, but should be able to afford, four or more pastors, sharing the ministry load in whatever way they and the church found to be effective and workable.

The stewardship problem is both the fault of church members and their pastors and teachers. Some few Christians really do not know the dimensions of their responsibility in giving. Even more members are confused by the debate over tithing. The greatest number, in all likelihood, are simply disobedient. They give stingily because their priorities are wrong. They may be over-committed and actually unable to tithe even if they wanted to. They may simply choose continually to spend their money on anything and everything else. Or, they may never even consider a level of giving that even approaches biblical standards for stewardship. They do not give proportionately. They do not give out of thoughtful gratitude. They do not give mindful of God's ownership and provision. They do not give with any awareness of accountability. They certainly do not tithe. Old jokes about dropping a single dollar in the offering plate come remarkably close to telling the truth about their giving habits.

And then, of course, as surveys have shown, many church members give absolutely nothing.

But if church members have a problem giving what they should, some pastors have failed to teach them adequately, firmly, and often, what the Bible says about Christian stewardship. Many pastors hate and detest having to preach about stewardship, and resist doing it except once a year when the budget is adopted, or in the fourth quarter when, if the church doesn't make up some of its deficit, some of its bills will go unpaid. Such neglect of essential teaching comes back to bite the pastor, usually sooner rather than later, because it helps perpetuate the poor giving of church members. And the church that cannot conceive of ever having a budget enabling them to do more than squeak by every year will not be easily convinced to envision adding a second pastor, or a third.

## A Slow Death

The church that develops more and more pastoral responsibilities without acquiring additional pastors to fulfill them is killing the one pastor they usually have. Denominations increasingly hold seminars and workshops on how pastors can better manage their time or otherwise deal with an increasing workload. But unless they figure out how they can add hours to the day and days to the week, denominations are going to fail in this strategy. Unless and until the concept of pastoral ministry is revolutionized, the growing expectation of pastors will continue to take its toll in the form of depression and anxiety, anger, neglected home life, broken marriages, shorter and shorter pastorates, thinner preaching and teaching, and burnout. The number of pastors leaving ministry altogether is staggering, and in many cases workload is one of the major causes.

Not only is the pastor hurt or defeated by this pressure, but the church invites its own destruction. Members disgruntled because of a pastor's failure to meet their needs typically do not console themselves by reasoning that he was overworked and couldn't tend to everything he was expected to do. They simply go elsewhere, where they believe the minister will be more attentive. The church that will not provide for its own ministries by staffing itself adequately will not reach or appeal to new people sufficiently to ensure its own growth. The result is often stagnation and decline, and eventually death.

*Case Study 5*

The new pastor of PQR Church in a Southern city came on board during a relocation program, as the church, about 900 members in size, was experiencing a period of modest growth. The new buildings were the talk of the town, and the church expected to acquire many new members because its new location was on a growing edge of town.

A planning group already at work when the pastor was called recommended the adoption of a half dozen new programs aimed at meeting "felt" needs of the new, upscale community into which the church was moving. The pastor was designated as the immediate planner, director or supervisor of all but one of these new programs (the exception was a child development center).

Within two years, a rapid influx of new members, most of them transfers from other congregations in the same denomination, expanded the membership by several hundred persons. Many of these new members were what might be gently called "high maintenance" in nature. The level of pastoral ministry responsibilities rose dramatically.

The pastor, now working about seventy hours per week, asked the appropriate groups of people to recommend that the church call an associate pastor. The deacons were not of the "ministering" sort, but the "managing" sort, and were not inclined to be retrained so as to give the pastor any help. Besides, the church had deep roots in a culture that expected the pastor and no one else to be present at every sick or troubled person's side. No deacon would do, except as auxiliary support.

The powers that be concluded that with the building program placing demands on the congregation, the church could not afford an additional staff member. In fact, they had already eliminated one support staff position to save money. The new members were not as good givers as the longstanding members were, though they were generally more wealthy. The newer members therefore added weight, but not resources, to the membership. The bottom line was that no help was coming soon for the pastor.

Meanwhile, the pastor's wife was pregnant with their third child. In the weeks leading up to the birth of what turned out to be a healthy boy, she felt increasingly neglected by her overworked husband. Finally, smart enough to realize that his home was more important than the church if push came to shove, the pastor cut back on his office hours, visitation, committee meetings, planning sessions, fellowships, counseling appointments and other responsibilities, and spent much more time with his wife and children. After the baby's birth, he continued this new routine, trying to work back into his schedule a little bit of the workload he had drastically reduced in his wife's third trimester of pregnancy.

By this time, however, in spite of the fact that the pastor was saving his marriage and fulfilling his primary duties to his family, the church was beginning to grumble. One Monday morning, a young deacon who had been known to make enigmatic remarks about ministers and church life came to see the pastor in his office. He "shared" some concerns with the pastor, relaying some of the criticism he had heard, but refusing to allow the pastor to know exactly who was complaining and precisely why. Then he concluded with this pronouncement: "Personally, I wouldn't be a pastor, because I believe a pastor ought to work eighty hours, six days a week, never take vacations, and spend every available minute out of the office pounding the neighborhood streets for Jesus."

The pastor thought he was exaggerating. He wasn't. He was deadly serious; and in the weeks after that private meeting, he drummed up support among other deacons, most of them young and feeling their oats. Within two months, four of them returned to the pastor and told him the deacons were prepared to present the church with a motion to dismiss him.

The pastor left the church after ascertaining that the threat was not a bluff, and after assessing his support at a bare majority. He went to work for a home improvement store temporarily, and eight years afterwards he was still not serving in a ministry position.

The church finished the exterior of its buildings, but two entire wings had to be left uncompleted because the membership took a sharp hit from the forced resignation of the pastor. Several of the more spiritually mature member families joined other churches in protest, leaving the church under the control of less mature leaders. A decade after the termination incident, the church continued to be stalled, and two new churches that were started in the area resulted in the shifting of attraction away from the PQR Church.

The PQR Church's burgeoning expectations of its pastor, followed by its refusal to provide additional ministerial staff to accomplish needed ministry, directly led to the injury done to the pastor, and the destructive effects experienced by the church.

By expecting too much of pastors, church members invite their own disappointment. But to add to the likelihood that they will be dissatisfied, they usually set up an organizational structure in the church that virtually guarantees the pastor will find it difficult to succeed—as we shall now see.

# 5

# Organizing for Failure

**Let all things be done decently and in order.**
**1 Corinthians 14:40**

A modern proverb has it that a camel is a horse put together by a committee. Unfortunately for many churches, they suffer from the odd designs of a similar creator. Churches have some of the most inefficient organizational philosophies in existence. And their eccentricities are not merely inconvenient: frequently they are disastrous to both the churches and the pastors who serve them.

The internal organization of churches is an area the New Testament does not address much. Some principles are given, but few details:

- We can gather with fair certainty that the elders/pastors/bishops (the terms are used synonymously in the New Testament) were accorded most of the leadership decisions. We know that the church as a congregation occasionally participated in major decisions. We discover that deacons were servants in practical matters. And we learn that many

people were active in preaching and witnessing besides the pastors.
- Aside from these general descriptions, we have specific guidelines given for only a few worship matters, such as the general content of worship, how to conduct the Lord's Supper, how to establish order in a service where participants are speaking in other languages, and perhaps a basic method of removing a member from the church.

However, the New Testament documents do not specify exactly how pastors in first century churches interrelated, what exact balance was achieved in any individual church between elders and congregation in decision making, or what procedures churches used in conducting everyday business.

Consequently, churches freely construct whatever operational organization they like. Most denominational churches have internal procedures like other churches in their families of faith, with minor differences in the smaller details. The range of differences is widest among congregational churches like Baptists, who are proud of their not having any bishop or presbytery dictating how they manage their affairs.

The result, however, is that organizational structures may be needlessly complex or frustratingly incomplete. While some churches seem corporately obsessive-compulsive about internal politics, others leave newcomers curious about how few written guidelines the church has.

Often, either the glut of guidelines or the dearth of directions is quite purposeful.

A study of various constitutions of Baptist churches is eye opening. Frequently, the reader can guess the history of a church from the language of its constitution. If an original document and a current version with all revisions are both available, sometimes the ability of a constitution to tell the church's story politically is remarkable.

Perhaps it could be argued that any constitution—say, for instance, that of the United States—would reveal such information. But church documents are often revised in the churning wake of recent crises, and their revisers are inclined to use blunt, unpolished language. As a result, the tale told between the lines is often crystal clear, and even funny—to disinterested parties, of course.

The histories these documents reveal are dotted with membership problems, staff improprieties, treasurer embezzlement, deacon immorality, election irregularities, committee ethical problems, pastoral dictatorship, feminist uprisings, or other situations. Events took place at some time in the church's past and were addressed in amendments to the church's constitution or bylaws. Occasionally, a church comes into existence out of a split or similar circumstance and those who write its founding documents do so with a bias developed out of their recent adversity.

Unfortunately, what sometimes happens when a church develops a reactionary constitution, is that it invents an organizational approach which, while it satisfies those on one side of a conflict, may cause difficulty for the church in the future—especially for staff members such as the pastor.

***Churches frequently organize by codifying a biased or unbiblical approach to pastoral leadership or decision-making that severely interferes with the pastor's ability to carry out his calling.***

Several traditional constitutional or bylaw provisions typically contribute to this problem many pastors face:

### A Supervisor Who Can Neither Hire nor Fire

In most cases, a pastor is acknowledged to be the supervisory head of the rest of the staff. Probably in more of these churches than not, however, the pastor is not permitted either to hire or fire staff members. This is true not only concerning ministerial staff (which is reasonable), but also support staff—secretaries, etc.

If a situation arises in which the staff cannot function effectively and amicably as a team because of a secretary's substandard performance or personal antagonism, the pastor cannot dismiss her. In many churches, he must call the personnel chairman and explain the problem. The personnel chairman then must call a meeting of his committee, and attempt to relay the pastor's report. Occasionally, but not always, the pastor is allowed to be part of such a meeting. Sometimes the laymen on the committee have the idea that the pastor's presence will prejudice them, or that he will pressure them, and consequently they prefer to meet by themselves. Or, they may simply have a territorial attitude and never invite him to attend. Either way, after the pastor has shared his concerns, they may insist on meeting in private to debate the issue and make a decision.

Sometimes the personnel committee wants to have a second meeting before making a decision. In between the two meetings, some of the committee members may interview the secretary to get her perspective. Here is where things get sticky.

The secretary may have been hired from within the church, a situation quite common in small, rural churches but not unusual anywhere. This person, usually a woman, may have served as secretary since just after the Great Flood, probably knows everybody in the church, and may have family ties to more than half the membership. By virtue of her frequent phone conversations on the job, very likely she has already carried on an effective campaign to garner support in the present situation, and she may also have planted subtle seeds suggesting that the pastor relates poorly to the staff and is either dictatorial or detached and uninvolved.

The personnel committee may sense, whether it discusses the matter openly or not, that the secretary is likely to have more popular support than the pastor, especially if he hasn't been at the church long. Despite their desire to help the pastor, the personnel committee may advise him to clear up any misunderstandings and work with the secretary.

Occasionally, the response of the personnel committee boils down to a basic valuation of two parties. They may, for instance, be less inclined to risk offending the family of the longtime, volunteer custodian, than of distressing the newly arrived pastor. In fact, while they may not consciously let such factors enter their deliberations, they may believe that a pastor is more easily replaced than a custodian. And depending on the local "market," they may be right.

Sometimes, such personnel situations are not remedied despite honest attempts by the pastor or other persons, and the conflict poisons the work of the entire staff.

Some pastors defend their church's designation of the personnel committee as the ones who hire and fire staff, because such a setup creates a buffer zone between the pastor and the church. Relieving him of the responsibility of having to terminate a position keeps him from absorbing the brunt of such changes.

The personnel committee can act with less individual negative impact for each of its members than the pastor can. The church may be upset by a dismissal it doesn't understand; but it may actually trust lay members more to act with sensitivity than it would the pastor.

Organizing this way sounds good in theory. But if the personnel committee is less than professional or has too little spiritual perception, as it frequently does, conflicts easily drag on far too long, the solution may be inadequate or totally inappropriate, and in either case both the church and the pastor may be hurt by what takes place.

## Case Study 6

Pastor Roth (not his real name) had just arrived at the TUV Church in a suburban neighborhood. TUV's pastor of nearly twenty-four years had moved to another state, after tearful goodbyes from a membership that almost universally adored him. Pastor Roth came to TUV realizing that he had a hard row to hoe, but he wasn't prepared for the resistance that greeted him.

During the week he moved in, he realized that his secretary, actually the only church secretary, was decidedly not thrilled by his coming. She had made up her mind that she did not like him. While Roth was moving in, some of his friends and fellow ministers dropped by to see his new situation. Several of them remarked to him in private as they were leaving, or called him later to say, that they were disturbed at how surly and acrid the secretary sounded as she spoke, both to them and to him.

Within a month, it became clear to Roth that the secretary was not softening. The reason also became clear, as Roth looked into the situation. The secretary had held her position for fourteen years, ever since becoming a Christian under the ministry of the former pastor. She had never known another pastor, and she had gotten very close to Roth's predecessor. She was a long way from recovering from the former pastor's departure. To make things worse, she was a person with a poor self-image with tendencies toward rapid anger, judgmental attitudes, and a sour disposition, except with close friends and family, with whom she displayed little of those characteristics. A psychological examination might have revealed bipolar disorder.

Roth hoped the situation would resolve itself. It didn't. He tried repeatedly to make friends with the secretary, but to no avail. Finally, he asked to meet with the personnel committee. The committee heard his gentle but deeply felt concerns. He didn't even ask the committee to dismiss the secretary, only to talk to her. But the committee comprised five people, all very good friends of hers. One was actually related to her—not a wise choice on the church's part, but not an unusual occurrence in churches where the greater part of the membership seems to be interrelated in some way.

Instead, the committee sidestepped the issue by simply asking for the secretary's view of staff relationships. Her response was mostly a summary of how Pastor Roth was not like the former pastor. The committee communicated to the pastor its opinion that he and the secretary needed to solve their differences, and they subtly implied that they did not intend to discipline or dismiss her. The rift was never healed, and the church's "in-family" approach added to the reasons the pastor eventually left the church for another position.

If the pastor, as the head of the staff, had the authority to hire and fire, situations like Pastor Roth's would not likely reach the extremes they did. Pastors are not eager to fire people, and if they were given the authority that supervisors in business situations usually have to hire and fire, pastors would not go about giddily dismissing people right and left. But the inability to take action when it really is necessary makes the pastor something of a toothless tiger where supervision is concerned.

Everyone would like to think of church staffs as having the feel of a warm family, sharing a passionate vision for the Christian faith, and never having a quarrel. No doubt, staff members, especially pastors, have the same idyllic dream. But staffs are composed of human beings. Perhaps more frequently than many people realize, problems exist and develop to the point of festering.

Why are pastors designated as the heads of their staffs, but not given the authority to fire if necessary, and to hire replacements? The chief reason is found in the basic philosophy of the church organization.

## Democratic Distrust

In many Protestant churches, particularly in congregationally governed churches, either pure democracy or representative democracy is the philosophy behind the organizational structure. Members want to be involved in deciding what happens. In medium to small-size churches where the membership is not only fairly constant, but often dominated by several families, positions of authority in one area of the church or another are passed around among a relatively small group, and most people continue to feel that they have ownership of their church's course and future.

The pastor, on the other hand, as wonderful as he may be as a preacher, and as admired for this or that, is not a member of the family. In most cases, "he isn't from around here," and the unspoken understanding is that he will be at the church only a while, and then move on. Exceptions exist, but merely prove the rule.

Consequently, churches do not generally fully surrender the business of managing the staff to the pastor. They want not only to continue to take a hands-on approach, but also to adopt a democratic distrust of granting executive authority to the pastor. Far from thinking it best for him to be spared the distastefulness of having to fire someone, or the trouble of having to hire someone, the real reason for the arrangement is that most churches really do not trust the pastor to do these things to their thorough satisfaction.

Essentially, many churches are committed to micromanaging the organization. In small churches, sometimes the entire congregation makes such decisions in business meetings. And the situation goes beyond hiring and firing. Often other committees such as buildings and grounds or maintenance will be involved in micro-managing other facets of staff affairs in the church office, further relegating actual business decisions to representative church groups, instead of the pastor and or other staff ministers.

A thoughtful study of church business practices once concluded that the reason so many churches get far behind in reaching the culture is that they are organized for sluggish response. Whereas businesses generally operate on a model that allows them to respond quickly to needs, churches are somewhat like ocean liners, taking vast stretches to make course changes. The insistence of the congregation or numerous committees on micro-managing staff affairs is an example of how the church is organized for failure, even if only partial or temporary in nature.

## You Lead, We'll Decide

The congregation's unwillingness to trust its pastor to thoroughly supervise the staff and office affairs is typically a part of a more overall policy in which the pastor is expected to lead but not allowed to make sufficient decisions to do so. A firmly established philosophy in business is that persons who have significant responsibility need authority equal to their tasks. Churches by and large have not learned the wisdom of this philosophy.

The pastor is expected to have a grand and glorious vision for the church. But he is not usually granted much authority to implement that vision without painstakingly selling it to the groups that control not just the purse strings of the church but the more basic decision as to whether the church will do a thing or not.

Usually, this group is either a church board or the "board of deacons," depending on the denomination or the individual polity of the church. The typical Baptist situation is that the deacons function as a board, reviewing all important business and either approving it unilaterally or passing it on to the church in conference with their affirmative vote. While situations vary widely, a very common scenario is that the pastor wishes to establish some new ministry, start a new event or class, adopt a new program, alter an existing program, or even just hold a revival meeting. Many deacon "boards" will insist on the pastor's presenting his ideas to them, after which they will vote to approve the matter. Even if the proposed matter does not cost any money, deacons often feel they should discuss and approve it—or not.

Even in matters not proposed by the pastor, many churches are organized in such a way that every business concern goes through the deacons:

- The nominating committee is charged with coming up with names for all church jobs and Sunday School positions. Before presenting a report to the church, however, many nominating committees are required by the church constitution to submit their report to the deacons, who review it and give their imprimatur.
- The personnel committee, which often is the real supervisor of the staff, in spite of what the constitution says, may itself be obliged to let the deacons make the final decision about hiring or firing.
- The buildings and grounds committee is often reduced to a group of volunteers who perform minor repairs and services themselves, but who present nothing to the church directly, but only through the deacons. In many

smaller churches the deacons themselves function as the buildings and grounds committee, eliminating the extra step, but creating another problem: absorbing yet another responsibility keeping deacons from being what they were meant to be in the church.
- The budget committee, if it is not also a subcommittee of the deacons, usually submits its proposed spending plan to the deacons for their stamp of approval.

And the list goes on. Deacons and some church members defend these procedures by saying things like, "the church trusts its deacons, and feels better about doing things if the deacons have passed them first." It is difficult to argue with such reasoning on the face of things, but the underlying attitude is one of distrust. The typical church does not trust non-deacon members to handle responsibility as much as it does deacons. What it is exactly that qualifies deacons to be better financial planners or personnel managers is never stated; but comparative distrust of non-deacons is obvious.

More interesting, however, is the implied distrust of pastors, as well, since they too are often required to present their plans and problems to the deacons. Why would a congregation not trust God-called, typically trained, devoted, lifelong servants in Christian ministry to make the necessary decisions to carry on their own ministries—ministries the church ostensibly called them to perform in the church? The question is baffling. Even more baffling is the question of why ministers, whose wise decisions and success in leading their churches have everything to do with their likelihood to stay in a church, or even to stay in the ministry altogether, would go about deliberately to make poor and irresponsible decisions that would guarantee their failure? It simply does not make sense to suggest that pastors cannot be trusted with the authority to carry out the ministries they have been called by God to accomplish.

Does this funneling of the bulk of church operations through deacons defeat the pastor or hurt the church? Absolutely it does, on both counts. As to the church:

- The church bogs down in the excessive review of matters that either don't need such review or that need to be acted on with dispatch.
- Good ideas are frequently watered down or even canceled in a process of evaluation that often subjects those ideas to less-than-spiritual criteria—such as when a visionary budget is cut by persons with little faith.
- Changes to the system are often vetoed by those holding the keys to the system.

And as to the pastor:

- He is defeated at many points in carrying out the goals of his ministry.
- He is stymied in his attempt to move the church from plateau to growth, from comfort to challenge, or from past-orientation to future-orientation.

- As the church fails to grow, minister or reach out because of sluggish or prejudicial politics, the pastor is linked by reputation with the negative results of his leadership, and the likelihood of his being attractive to another church, when the time comes for him to seek a change, is lessened.
- In severe cases, the control group of a church may so strongly oppose the pastor's initiatives that it polarizes the membership over him, forcing a crisis in his ministry that may lead to his ouster.

## The Tyranny of Pure Democracy

In churches where control rests in a church board or the deacons, sometimes the congregation is only minimally involved. Some very large churches avoid church votes on all but the most significant of decisions, allowing the deacons, for instance, to run everything else. Such church polity greatly resembles a representative republic, the form of government found in the United States.

Other churches, however, while giving great authority to the deacons to review the work of most committees and of the pastor as well, still want to have monthly or quarterly business conferences in which the congregation as a whole can vote on everything from purchasing new flower arrangements to buying a new copier to repainting the baptistry to paving the parking lot. In many cases, it matters not to these churches that many expenditures and actions are anticipated in the passage of an annual budget, or that committees exist in the appropriate area to spend those monies, or that the finance committee exists to handle many other matters not specifically planned for. The church still wants to have someone "bring it to the congregation," so they may debate it and vote on it.

Baptists as a group value their historical assumption that democracy is the proper polity for a church. Baptists, therefore, are among the most vociferous proponents of the vote of the congregation. (This book has occasionally addressed the situations of other denominations, some of which also have many democratic features about their church governance, at least at the local church level.) All congregational churches favor the right of everyone in the congregation to be involved in the decision-making process.

But sometimes, especially as a church grows, insisting on retaining the pure democracy of congregational debate on practically every issue endangers the progress of the body. Ministries can be paralyzed or detoured by their subjection to the vagaries of pure democracy.

Pure democracy, also called direct democracy, is a system in which the entire body has a vote on everything and each vote is equal. It's also a recipe for disaster. The classic illustration—a decidedly blunt exaggeration used for many years and predating me—posits a group of three unrelated persons, two men and one woman, stranded on a desert island. They agree that until they are rescued they will make decisions about their life on the island by democratic vote. All goes well until one of the men proposes that he and the other man should both have sex with the woman. Putting it to a vote, the two men vote yea, and the woman loudly votes nay. Consequently, she loses and they prevail upon her. The vote was democratic; but no one will conclude that it was just.

Many such examples could be described. The great potential of pure democracy for injustice is why the United States does not have a pure democracy, but a representative, constitutional democracy, in which government is based on law, and is administered by representatives elected by the people. Everyone gets a vote on his representatives. But those representatives are the only ones to vote on government procedures, and even they are bound by the constitution, an intensely studied, painstakingly written, overwhelmingly adopted body of principles that form the foundation of the country.

Most churches having a somewhat democratic form of governance also have a constitution or set of bylaws giving foundational guidance. The better and fuller constitutions and bylaws lay out a plan for committees and individuals elected by the body to be trusted to carry out portions of the church's business as a whole.

Those persons and teams of people are like automotive assembly line workers. In some churches a power group subverts the constitutional process—it runs down the assembly line and does every person's job for him. In other churches the constitution is simply ignored by the entire congregation—the auto workers do their jobs however they feel at the moment. Who would expect a car that came from that plant to be anything but a lemon?

Whether power groups dominate or constitutions are simply ignored, the church may succeed in mostly maintaining the status quo, to its own eventual destruction. Additionally, the church may wound pastors and other ministers who valiantly attempt to lead them to liberation and growth through change.

## Getting it Backwards

In many cases, the ultimate reason the typical power group— deacons—insist that not only church committees but the pastor himself channel his proposals and business through them is that many deacons have a backwards concept of their role in relation to the pastor. While deacons in the Bible were chosen to help the pastors, many deacons today are convinced that the pastor works for them.

It is an all-too-common experience: the pastor attempts to lead the church into uncharted territory, because he is convinced the church cannot grow and will not survive without taking bold initiatives. The deacons, however, field numerous complaints from members who for one reason or another object to the church's growth or change. Several related events escalate tensions until the deacons, perhaps led internally by a smaller, activist core, issue an ultimatum: the pastor should move immediately, or resign immediately, or they will present a motion to the church that he be dismissed.

While examples of this generalized story are exasperatingly common, let us consider a story gathered recently from a wounded pastor.

## Case Study 7

Pastor Jimmy Wedford (again, not his real name) moved into the WXY Church in an old suburban neighborhood. Jimmy had been at a previous church for eight years, and took the pastorate of a church of similar size, putting his family near his wife's ailing parents. For the first time during Wedford's ministry, he and his wife bought a house.

Barely a year into his pastorate, things were not going well. Wedford discovered that at least twenty percent of the members who had been present the day of the vote to call him as pastor had abstained from the vote. His source for this information, a reliable person with no axe to grind, recognized from a wealth of experience that these people were a closely knit group, and she believed that they had opposed Wedford's call from the very first. The reason seemed to be that Wedford's known style of worship leaned toward the contemporary, while the group preferred a traditional approach.

The group's abstaining from the vote did not, however, indicate that they intended to go along with the majority. Instead, they were active in opposing the pastor's leadership from the first. Whether or not they had meetings to decide how best to defeat pastor Wedford is irrelevant. Their actions began to accomplish that goal just the same. What made their efforts very effective was that many of them were core members of the church, and part of the power structure, the deacons.

First, the church needed a minister of music, and had waited until the pastor arrived to select a team to search for one. The dissident deacon group influenced the nomination of the search committee, and several of them were on it. They recommended a man slightly older than the pastor, one who preferred traditional music, with an occasional modern song thrown in as a bone to the younger set. The procedure set forth in the church's constitution was silent on pastoral involvement in the selection of a minister of music, and the committee gave the pastor only a brief opportunity to meet the candidate and assess the potential working relationship. The candidate was called, and almost immediately Pastor Wedford realized the partnership was not going to work.

Meanwhile, Wedford was attempting to get a prayer ministry started. Recognizing the need to get the deacons involved in this ministry, he had introduced the plan to them several months before starting it. The deacons were a business-oriented group who had adopted a "family ministry plan" to appease the former pastor, but had never done anything with it. Wedford attempted to convince them to be the core group of the prayer program, on the theory that if the church saw the deacons praying, the church itself would be led to pray. On several occasions in meetings, deacons gave indications that they thought favorably of the idea. The chairman said several times that he was sure they were all behind it.

When the prayer events began, however, no deacons showed up. After three of the bimonthly prayer meetings had come and gone, the pattern was clear: deacons had no interest in the *pastor's* prayer meeting.

The deacons, however, did have an interest in the pastor himself. Wedford noticed over a period of weeks that several deacons seemed to be in rotation making visits to the church office. On what turned out to be fairly thin premises, one would come by to check on the office computers or copier. Another would come by to check on various maintenance issues, always close to the offices. Wedford was very systematic and regular about office hours, and couldn't imagine that the deacons were checking up on him, but essentially they were, and they were attempting to engage the church secretary in casual conversation designed to acquire information that might be useful to them in finding fault with Wedford's staff relationships or daily performance.

The pastor managed to act as if nothing were wrong, for a while. Eventually, however, he began to be bothered immensely by this effort to gather information to use against him. One day he sat down with the secretary to ask her candidly what kind of things deacons wanted to talk to her about. She said she had noticed they were especially curious about where he went when he left the office, and whether or not she knew where he was (she did), and other related topics.

While the deacons were resisting spiritual activities, other dissidents were planning an annual homecoming event, and leaving the pastor out of it entirely. They had even invited a special speaker, and informed the pastor of the plan after the fact. Pastor Wedford found it impossible to hide his shock when told, and the members who informed him saw clearly that he was insulted and proceeded to publicize his reaction throughout the church—especially, of course, to the core group of dissidents. They showed themselves to be gifted in the political art of "the spin." They managed to convince people that the pastor's being upset at their having usurped his pulpit privilege was somehow an offense on his part, not theirs.

A half dozen other little things took place involving Wedford and the original group that had abstained from the vote to call him. And all along, as Wedford learned later, deacons had gathered without him in meetings called by the dissident group. Finally, their ducks in a row, the deacons sent emissaries to Wedford to deliver an ultimatum. They would call a meeting of the church to vote him out, if he did not resign first.

Wedford did not resign. The church was full the day the deacons called a meeting, its normally empty pews occupied by usually absent members. Though a few persons rose to ask tearfully what the pastor had done to deserve being voted out, the ballot was about sixty percent to dismiss him.

A month after Wedford left the church, he called the secretary to inquire about something he may have left in her office. While they were talking, she told him again how much she thought of him and how seriously she was considering quitting because of what had taken place. And she said the deacon chairman had been by the office that morning to "give her direction." She also believed he had come to reinforce the concept that the deacons were right and the pastor was incompetent and not right for the church. And while repeating a list of niggling irritations about Wedford, he mentioned a particular time when she, the secretary, had called him, the deacon chairman, to relay a message from the pastor about a church member in the hospital. The chairman concluded his complaint to the secretary by saying, "He didn't call me, himself, *and I'm his boss!*"

Interviewed later, Wedford said that years of experience had convinced him that an astounding number of deacons *believed* they were the pastor's boss, but that never had he heard one of them *say* so, and do it so bluntly and unashamedly.

Deacons who have things backwards, believing that the pastor works for them, frequently become a formidable force against pastoral leadership. The church that organizes itself so that deacons supervise the pastor is a church that has prejudiced its future toward an adversarial relationship with him. By biblical precedent and the dynamic of his calling the pastor has been placed in the church to lead, not to be led around. And the church that either asks or simply lets its deacons rise to a position of authority over pastors has become party to the epidemic of injurious machinations resulting in a widening stream of forced terminations and many more situations of misery and health-threatening stress faced by pastors.

The church where deacons truly consider themselves servants, not rulers, is comparatively rare. Even as the exception, however, these churches and their deacons stand out starkly as models.

Likewise, rare is the church that has escaped, or blessedly never had, the sluggish bureaucracy that is the bane of the body of Christ. These few churches, too, should be the models for churches to come. Perhaps if healthy churches plant enough other churches to replace those now dying, the new model—which is really the old model—will prevail.

The church that unwittingly has set itself up for failure has more than an organizational problem, however. At root, its problem is spiritual. We turn now to investigate how the church may frustrate the pastor's attempt to lead because its people largely are not inclined to follow.

# 6

## The Church That Will Not Be Led, The Pastor Who Will Not Be Followed

**The days of punishment are coming, the days of reckoning are at hand. Let Israel know this. Because your sins are so many and your hostility so great, the prophet is considered a fool, the inspired man a maniac. The prophet, along with my God, is the watchman over Ephraim, yet snares await him on all his paths, and hostility in the house of his God.**
**Hosea 9:7-8 NIV**

Who does Christ want leading his churches? Models of Israel's leadership in the Old Testament and the church's leadership in the New seem to answer the question fairly clearly. We have already seen that the Bible testifies to God's choice of elders—men of spiritual maturity and divine calling—to "have the rule" in his church. The New Testament also shows some level of participation by the entire church in significant decisions. The biblical examples are not much more specific than that.

Local churches and groups of churches have developed a wide variety of strategies to integrate the authority of their elders with congregational involvement. Some churches have acknowledged little other source of leadership than their pastors or priests: such systems tend toward autocracy. At the other end of the spectrum, other churches have eliminated most of their pastors' authority in favor of congregational politics: these churches reduce the pastor's authority, if he has any at all, to mere administration.

This book makes no argument for a dictatorship by the pastor; but neither does it go along with deleting crucial authority from the pastor's role. His role must be significant, because his responsibility under God is significant.

***Many churches are currently in crisis because they have largely positioned themselves against their pastor's legitimate, authoritative role, jeopardizing their own success in finding God's direction.***

The pastor's authority in the church consists in a role that has always been associated with that authority: leadership. Through his prophetic ministry—preaching—and even through his interpersonal ministry, the pastor is to be the principal leader of the church. The very concept of a pastor, which means "shepherd," is that he leads the sheep. The sheep need to be led to spiritual food, led to reviving waters, led to rest, led into the future. There is no question that leadership is one of the key functions of the pastor in Christ's plan for the church.

Look at a bit of history about how this leadership of God's flock developed.

## The Prophet-Leader Model

From the time of Moses to the coming of Jesus, God's preferred plan to lead Israel was to communicate his word through persons of his choosing who in turn would communicate God's message and will to the people. They would serve as both prophets and leaders. Beginning with Moses, God gifted some to be prophets for his chosen flock. In the period of the judges, those select individuals were God's spokesmen as well as governors. God's plan was simple: to reveal to these called persons what his people needed to know; for these prophet-leaders in turn to proclaim God's will and lead God's people in doing it; and for the people then to follow those God gave them as leaders.

The young nation Israel weakened that plan by insisting on having a king like the countries around them. Even then, God had his prophets select and anoint the first king, and the one who replaced him (because, as God had said, kings would go astray). Eventually, however, royal succession led to many kings who "did not what was right in the sight of the Lord," and they led the country into a deep nightmare of sin and judgment that lasted many generations.

The prophets who spoke the word of the Lord to the nation included: Nathan, who kept David on his toes; Jonah, who also did mission work in Nineveh; Amos, Hosea, Isaiah, Jeremiah, Ezekiel, and many others. About four hundred years before Christ, the prophet Malachi preached and labored among the Israelites after their captivity had ended; but when he was gone there was not another prophet until John the Baptist, and then Jesus Christ. During their entire history, Israel and Judah had kings, high priests and princes of all kinds; but no one spoke for the Lord the way the prophets did. God preferred to lead his chosen people into righteousness and on to glory through these prophets' ministries.

A new age began when Jesus established a new covenant through his blood and began to build his church. God's kingdom now was not limited to the one nation through whom he had chosen to reveal himself, but was extended to people everywhere who would accept his Lordship in their lives through the divinely anointed King, Jesus Christ. Each church that sprang up wherever people believed the gospel acknowledged Jesus as Lord and themselves as his surrendered subjects. And in each of those churches Christ himself placed people to mediate his leadership of that particular flock:

> **It was he who gave some to be apostles, some to be prophets, some to be evangelists, and some to be pastors and teachers, to prepare God's people for**

**works of service, so that the body of Christ may be built up.
Ephesians 4:11 NIV**

The prophets spoken of by Paul seem to have functioned in the first century church primarily as conduits of divine messages to the churches in the transition period between Pentecost and the end of the apostolic era. In other words, they spoke the word of God "live" when there was yet to be a completed, written New Testament of God's self-revelation. By around the end of the first century, the documents we know as the New Testament were complete, and we have no records of there being prophets in all the churches: the highly specialized work they did was now obviated by the completion of the Bible.

But the role of the prophet for the church had hardly disappeared. Now that the written word of God was complete, its proclamation, with all the authority possessed by the prophets of old, was in the purview of the pastor-teachers Paul spoke of in Ephesians 4—the elders who "labour in the word and doctrine" (1 Tim. 5:17). As Paul stated conclusively to Titus, "These things speak, and exhort, and rebuke with all authority (Tit. 2:15).

### The Pastor as Prophet

The pastor of the New Testament church is the spiritual inheritor of the role of prophet to God's people. To the extent that other pastors (elders) in a local church minister in "the word and doctrine," they too share the prophetic role. The ministry of some pastor-prophets goes beyond the borders of their church fields and makes an impact on a region, a country, or beyond, and speaks to an entire generation. But every church has its own prophet, so to speak, in the one who stands before it and faithfully proclaims God's word.

The pastor thus serves a dual role as both shepherd and prophet. Every church knows this in theory, for every church's pastor search committee at some point talks with a prospective pastor about the two roles of pastor and preacher. They know the pastor will preach and lead; but they also look for someone who will feed and comfort.

The problem with many local churches is that what they know in theory they do not practice in fact. Perhaps there have always been churches here and there that had a problem with accepting spiritual authority; but at the turn of the twenty-first century the problem has become a pestilence.

Interviews with pastors and other church leaders indicate they recognize a spirit of rebellion and defiance permeating growing numbers of churches. Denominational leaders can show a frightening statistical curve representing churches that are eating pastors alive and pastors who are reeling and sometimes leaving the ministry behind in their discouragement.

The prophet Hosea spoke to a similar condition of pervasive rebellion against spiritual leadership. He didn't merely describe the situation: he prophesied that because of their rebellion, Israel was going to be punished. It is hermeneutically sound to apply the general principle of that prophecy of Hosea to God's people today. The ramifications for churches are foreboding.

Essentially, Hosea said:

*"You will be punished because you have been hostile to the preacher-leaders God has sent you. I gave them to you to lead you to me, and you have persecuted them and constantly sought ways to get rid of them."*

To translate Hosea's pronouncement into words that reflect the current crisis, he described the situation of *the church that will not be led, and the pastor who will not be followed.* In such circumstances, both sides lose: the church loses because it closes itself off to the purpose of God and chooses a path of self-determination often ending in a long, slow death; and the pastor loses in the sense that he is defeated in his goals and deterred in his calling, sometimes being displaced along with his family.

## The Church that *Will Not* be Led

Churches come in all varieties, just like the buildings they meet in. Some churches are alive and vibrant, while others are dead and cold. Some are involved in ministry, others are detached. And some churches honor and follow the leaders God sends them, while others either ignore or actively resist being led, especially if the direction is toward growth or change. Some churches, in an overall sense, simply *will not be led.*

Granted, almost every church in this quagmire (and it *is* a quagmire) includes people who do accept spiritual leadership—who even crave it. But in some churches these folks are in a decided if not an miniscule minority. Instead, these churches are dominated by persons who persistently resist being led almost anywhere by their pastors, especially if it isn't somewhere they didn't already want to go before he arrived on the scene.

The church that will not be led is typically characterized by several conditions:

- It is at least two generations old; that is, it was founded by the grandparents of young adults in the church today, or by a generation prior to them.
- It is dominated by several extended families, who populate the various committees and councils.
- It has a congregational authority structure in which deacons are the designated board of directors, whether stated in a constitution or not.
- It has had one or more pastors perhaps in a previous generation who have catered to the dominant families and to the deacons as board members so as not to rock the boat, thus reaffirming an indigenous leadership structure that usually becomes antagonistic to change or aggressive pastoral leadership.

Obviously, variations exist on this theme. Some very new churches already have a problem with stubbornness. And some churches have had no pastors who aided and abetted their march toward hardheadedness; however, the church arrived at its chosen destination anyway. But the general description of "the church that will not be led" fits so many of the congregations under consideration that almost any pastor who has ever been in one of those churches will think someone has been surreptitiously investigating his struggles in order to profile problem churches.

In what ways does the spirit of rebellion evidence itself in these churches? Here are some typical manifestations:

- ***Indifference:*** The church as a whole ignores the plea of the pastor to be involved in outreach to its immediate community, in spite of the fact that some or many members live in that community. The pastor may preach on outreach, evangelism, and the need of ministry; he may point out the need of reaching the community simply to survive as a church. But church members say things like, "People know where we are and could come if they wanted to," or even, "They wouldn't be interested in our church." This manifestation is often prevalent in communities where economic, racial, and/or social transition has taken place.
- ***Inflexibility:*** The church has experienced a decline in the success of its educational programs, largely due to its insistence on doing things exactly as the previous generation (or the one before it) did them. Yet,

presented with leadership toward changing its approach, it appeals to the well-known seven last words of the church: "We never did it that way before."

- ***Ineducable-ness:*** The church has developed traditions that go counter to proven principles of church growth, but the members refuse to believe either in the truth of those principles or that such principles would work in their case. For instance, consistent research shows that small Sunday School classes (or any kind of small group with outreach as one of its goals) grow faster than large ones. But in spite of a pastor's attempts to educate Sunday School classes or even teachers and Sunday School directors in the proven research, the individuals involved turn a deaf ear. Sometimes the reason is no more complicated than that the individuals whom change would affect would be upset if their classes were split and they had fewer subjects in their Sunday School class kingdoms. Sometimes the problem is conceptual: teachers often associate large class size with success, or feel their social events will be less exciting if fewer people are involved.
- ***Intractability:*** The church experiences the continual need of more communication between its various organizations and leaders. The pastor introduces the idea of a church council—something too few churches have, or have a functioning version of. But because the inherent role of a church council conflicts with the entrenched power structure, those involved in that structure, along with their families and friends,

convince the church that the creation of a church council would be generally unwise. In severe cases, in order to marshal the troops, power brokers may suggest the pastor is trying to take over the church.

- *Inattentiveness:* Church traditions sometimes conflict with scripture. Pastors often try to lead churches away from unbiblical habits and activities through gentle but forthright teaching. But if old habits die hard, old church habits are downright deathless. Churches, however, are not immune to death, and some had rather die than kill the traditions that threaten them.

The classifications of a church's rebellious nature can be reduced to these or a few other types; but the variations on these types of rebellion against leadership are innumerable.

## The Pastor who *Will Not* be Followed

Looked at as a pastor's particular problem, the situation seems to revolve around recurring negative behavior on the part of individuals and dysfunctional behavior on the part of the church as a family.

- *Disinterest:* Preaching in general is ignored. Many pastors have experienced this problem, and know neither how it developed nor how to solve it. The fact is that in many churches preaching is an activity expected in a worship service but which few pay close attention to. Many churches expect preaching to be highly emotional but mostly to validate things the congregation already feels. Many church members—and therefore their churches as a whole—have little to no interest in learning anything new through preaching, and refuse to be challenged to think, even less to study on their own, and least of all to actually change their minds.

- ***Disingenuousness:*** Despite the claims of some church members that they like having their toes stepped on, the prevailing attitude is quite the opposite. Often, preachers are expected to mirror the congregation's prejudices, not confront them. When pastors attempt to challenge moral and ethical evil outside the church, church members cheer. When pastors attempt to confront the church about its own sins, they jeer. Preachers tell jokes about church members who say, "You've quit preachin' and gone to meddlin'." But the reality is no joke. The pastor who experiences the church whose members' faces are set like flint toward worldly ways has two options: continue confronting them and pay the price in constant skirmishing and possibly forced termination; or compromise if only by remaining silent, and pay the price in lost integrity and perhaps the discipline of God.
- ***Complacency:*** The church not only doesn't have a mission statement, but does not want one. A pastor recently related how he went to talk with a pastor search committee from a sizeable church. Noting their apparent stagnation in a place of more than modest growth, he asked about their mission statement. The blank stares

gave him his answer. Further discussion convinced him that they were not interested in making an impact on the community, but mostly saw their goal as acquiring enough members chiefly to sustain their ongoing social life within the church as an organization. Their resources were poured into developing the fun and fellowship of the current members and those who might be accepted in the future for purposes of canceling the effects of attrition. A look at their history showed that their previous two pastors had come and gone in just a few years when they were unable to lead the church into an outreach and ministry mentality.

- *Control:* In practice, the church members reveal the working belief that the church belongs to them. In theory they may confess emptily that the church belongs to Jesus Christ. But when called on to adopt ministries that are biblical, or to change activities that are not biblical, or to trust their pastor's urgent conviction that the Lord is saying, "This is the way: walk ye in it" (Is. 30:21), they bristle. The pastor becomes an outsider who after all doesn't understand or value the traditions of the church, and who has a personal agenda that is merely dictatorial.

*Case Study 8*

Mike Shepherd (not his real name) came as pastor to ZYX Church, joining a small staff. Upon arriving, he was given a long list of traditions the church followed. Literally, he was given the list in writing.

The church had a Halloween party.
The church always had a visit from Santa Claus.
The church put a Christmas tree in the auditorium.
The church had an Easter egg hunt.
The children had an Easter parade across the platform during a worship service.
The church had a homecoming celebration every year. On and on the list went. The pastor said that not only was the list long, but it was delivered with an emphatic manner by the one who brought it, as if it were a set of ultimatums: either we observe all these things the way we always have, or you leave.

Shepherd didn't have a serious problem with annual homecomings, though he wondered about their intrinsic value. But he did have convictions about mixing spiritual emphases with worldly ones at Christmas, Easter and Halloween. As many pastors these days, Shepherd had come to question personally the appropriateness of such things as Halloween celebrations at church. While he didn't think they were demonic necessarily, he was troubled about children's becoming confused by a dual message: we reject superstition and we don't believe the devil is a joke, but we celebrate superstitions galore and make light of demonic things at Halloween.

Shepherd spoke briefly to the planning committee for the Halloween party about his views, attempting in the most respectful way to influence them toward a different direction for that fall's observance.

They would have none of it. It was all in fun, anyway,

they said. After all, they themselves had done such things as children, and it wasn't fair to cheat the children of the same fun. Shepherd said later that he suspected this was the real source of the parents' determination to have Halloween with all the trappings: they were reliving their own youth.

Not having learned anything from his experience at Halloween, Shepherd tried again at Christmas. While he never once intimated that people should dispense with Santa Claus at home, he did hold the line at having Saint Nick come into the worship service, although the practice was deeply ingrained. Not a few murmurs went through the church about his interference with tradition.

But when Shepherd had the audacity to approach the individual who had always decorated the main church bulletin board seasonally, and asked her to select a crucifixion-resurrection theme instead of pictures of Easter eggs, he had pushed too far. The decorator was one of those multiply involved individuals who have inestimable influence, and whom everyone wants on his side. Shepherd had just crossed the wrong woman. He had done it in the nicest possible way (according to him); but she was unteachable, and intractable. And as far as she was concerned, the pastor was at the church on borrowed time.

It turned out that he was.

*Case Study 9*

Rod had been at the WVU Church for fifteen years and had struggled uphill against spiritual apathy and myopia through all of them. Not a confrontational person by nature, Rod had early adopted the tack of gentle, almost imperceptible teaching aimed at opening minds and eventually changing them.

Where the church seemed less concerned about the neighborhood around them than a nearby upscale development, Rod preached on love and ministry to the hurting. He and an associate personally won and brought into the church several neighborhood residents. However, not only did precious few people follow his example, but the rest virtually shunned the newcomers. Finally, one of the deacons verbalized the church's spirit to the pastor: "Bringing in some single mommas and such is fine; but what we need is to go after those families over there [in the upscale development] with children and money, or our church is going to stay in the red."

Rod's jaw almost dropped. While it was common wisdom that many church members preferred "normal" families with money to their counterparts, he had never heard anyone actually say it—with or without apology. Apparently, his pulpit leadership, personal conversations and deacon-meeting talks had gone in one proverbial ear and exited the other at full speed.

## The Reason for Having a Pastor

Pastors who, in attempting to lead their churches, have experienced severe resistance (and that's most pastors) may be inclined to ask what the church wanted a pastor for anyway. In some cases, the pastor is followed in virtually no direction he attempts to go. In others, the pastor must work slowly behind the scenes, convincing deacons that his ideas are theirs. Then he must wait for the ideas to work their way through the maze of lazy discussions, politics, and finally a captious or fussy debate in a church conference. After finally passing, the new measure or program may have lost its timely edge or effectiveness in a rapidly developing situation—such as adopting a ministry to keep youth from leaving the church because they feel there is nothing for them there.

It may not be too simplistic to say that some churches acquire pastors mostly to administer the programs they want perpetuated. They don't want any of them changed, and they don't want to add any; they just want someone to run the ones they have.

In other churches, mostly smaller ones where for years the same people have run all of the few programs they have, the church wants a pastor mostly because nobody else wants to preach. That's a skill they don't possess. Basically, they are engaged in subcontracting pulpit duties.

The bottom line is that some churches are looking for someone to be a figurehead, to appear to lead them, but actually to follow them as they, the church, exert the control and define the direction. This strategy requires that they find pastors who subscribe to the theory of leadership that says, 'Find a crowd going somewhere, and get out in front of it.' While a few pastors exist who operate on that philosophy, not many do. And because most don't, they run into trouble the more they attempt actually to lead their churches, much less to do so aggressively.

Jesus once said something interesting about people's response to both John the Baptist and him:

> **To what, then, can I compare the people of this generation? What are they like? They are like children sitting in the marketplace and calling out to each other: 'We played the flute for you, and you did not dance; we sang a dirge, and you did not cry.'**
> **(Luke 7:31-32) NIV**

If people expected to play a tune and have John or Jesus dance to it, they were seriously mistaken. John had a calling of God as a prophet, and a message to preach, and he was going to preach it whether people liked it or not, though it would cost him his head. Jesus had a mission in the world and he was going to accomplish it no matter what enemies he made, though it would get him crucified.

The problem in most churches where there is strife between church members and pastors is not pastors failing to do what God called them to do, but church members failing to follow leadership and neglecting to respect and heed the word of God and the vision imparted to the ones God has sent to guide them.

Paul warned Timothy about the emergence of such church members (whom he may not have intended to say were actually Christians):

> **For the time will come when they will not endure sound doctrine; but after their own lusts shall they heap to themselves teachers, having itching ears.**
> **2 Tim. 4:3**

Paul's envisionment goes beyond mere resistance to leadership; but certainly the principle he taught Timothy is the same one at work in churches that *will not* be led: they do not listen to the ones God sends to lead them. Instead, out of their own desires they formulate their plans, and secure preachers who will tamely assist them in achieving those plans, while saying all the things the church wants to hear.

The tragic thing about this dysfunctional development among church families is that it identifies them as churches desperately needing strong, biblical leadership to teach them and lead them into spiritual maturity and productivity.

Two pastors were discussing a particularly troubled church looking for a pastor. The first pastor had been considered, and said he was likely to turn down the committee's invitation. The second sympathized with him, but added thoughtfully, "But you know, *somebody* has to be their pastor." A simple but profound response expresses the dilemma: these churches desperately need strong pastors with vision; but they are likely to try to run off such a man before he can do them any good.

More and more, however, pastors are becoming leery about participating in the game many churches play. The stakes are too high for their own calling, and the churches themselves need to be jolted out of their stubbornness. Consequently, many pastors are paying the price personally. If they thought their own sacrifice might eventually be part of a church's repentance and awakening, they might be encouraged to press on despite the loss. If they knew that many of these churches would never change, but would go on resisting the Holy Spirit and stoning the Stephens God sends them, then many pastors would stay away from those flocks altogether. But because pastors cannot know beforehand which churches are which, they risk their ministries every time a search committee phones and says, "The church voted to call you. Will you come?"

Despite a church's resistance to leadership, its need for it does not diminish. However, as we shall see next, in becoming skeptical of ministerial leadership, a church may follow other leaders who really do not have the sheep's best in mind.

# 7

## Too Many Chiefs

**Not many of you should presume to be teachers, my brothers, because you know that we who teach will be judged more strictly.**
**James 3:1 NIV**

An old and now politically incorrect adage aptly expresses the condition of an organization having an overabundance of competition for leadership: "Too many chiefs and too few Indians." We could change the names to protect the easily offended: "Too many cooks spoil the broth." A Korean version of the same truth is interesting: "Too many boatmen send the boat up the mountain."

Obviously, human beings have noticed that when too many people try to control outcomes, outcomes suffer. Why haven't more people realized that this truth applies to churches as well as other organizations? In fact, even casual observation suggests that churches suffer more from too many would-be chiefs than almost any other entity, except perhaps Congress.

The term "power struggle" is tragically familiar to Christian circles. It is the most highly reported reason for church difficulties including those that end with the forced termination of the church's pastor. And it isn't only pastors who characterize churches' problems as revolving around power struggles: it's also some church members. A Sunday School teacher recently commented about her own church's woes, "It's power politics. So many people think they should run the church. It makes me sick at heart."

Power struggles do more than make spiritually sensitive people sick at heart. They make the entire church sick spiritually. The result is tragic:

*The church that vies with its own pastor for leadership chips or even flails away at the pastor's implementation of his vision until it defeats him, and in the process it participates in its own destruction.*

## Warnings from Scripture

James counseled churches to avoid the pitfall of having too many people claiming authority. He used the Greek word *didaskaloi,* which means "teacher"; but also it often described the kind of person who led disciples and was looked to as an authority. This was the sense intended by the King James translators when they rendered James's word "master" in James 3:1. James was not talking about Sunday School teachers. He was talking about people who seek positions of authority in churches as teacher-leaders.

This verse certainly applies to those who seek to be

preachers or pastors when they have not been divinely called. But it also applies to those who while not seeking the office of pastor do, in fact, want the recognition and privilege that go with leadership positions, and may make themselves out to be teachers—if only of tradition or common wisdom—who should be followed. The term often applied is "power brokers."

James warned Christians about presuming to have been authorized to gather followings in the church. He referred to God's intended leaders by saying, "We who teach will be judged more strictly," meaning by comparison to those who follow. Interestingly, James's warning is not expressed in terms of what ill effects the church will suffer for having too many teachers. Instead, he cleverly couches the caveat in terms of what will happen to the would-be teacher himself. If the power broker isn't interested in how his political machinations will hurt the church, perhaps he will think of how he may hurt himself.

James was not alone in pointing out the early emergence of power brokers in the church. John in his third letter mentioned a man named Diotrephes who had virtually taken over a church:

> **I wrote to the church, but Diotrephes, who loves to be first, will have nothing to do with us. So if I come, I will call attention to what he is doing, gossiping maliciously about us. Not satisfied with that, he refuses to welcome the brothers. He also stops**

**those who want to do so and puts them out of the church.**
**3 John 9-10**

John wrote to Gaius at this unidentified church, asking him personally to show hospitality to some traveling missionaries coming his way, since the church itself had not welcomed them. The problem was particularly this man Diotrephes, about whom John made three charges:

- He set himself against the leaders God sent—in this case, John himself, still an apostle and still having authority to guide various churches as an elder (v.9).
- He misrepresented the words and leadership of John so as to erode his credibility and thwart his plans (v.10).
- He attempted to manipulate members, if necessary by intimidation, and to control outcomes according to his personal wishes (v.10).

These charges—which constitute accurate observations because of their inclusion in scripture by the pen of John the apostle—describe the quintessential power broker in a church.

## Who Are They?

Who are these teachers, these masters, these chiefs who seek power and leadership? And how do they differ from the normal internal leadership every church needs?

Power brokers are generally distinguished from merely influential, internal leaders by looking at three factors: connections, attitudes, and goals.

*Connections:* A person with no connections, no network of pliable friends and co-leaders, is not likely to be able to wield much authority. Power brokers nurture their networks through frequent, confidential conversations, and use their gifts of persuasion to win converts to their philosophical viewpoints. They may have a network previously in place, such as community friendships of longstanding, or extensive family ties. The power broker has learned how to use relationships to his advantage. While networking is beneficial when used for benevolence, it can easily be used as a support system for manipulating an organization for illegitimate goals.

*Attitudes:* While a person may have an extensive network of friends simply because he makes friends easily and is well liked, the power broker has an attitude that identifies him or her as more than just socially successful.

The power broker is usually opinionated. While everyone has opinions, the power broker is more forceful with his opinions, and may be engaged easily in arguing about them. Some of these persons are the easily recognizable, ornery individuals who because of their lack of subtlety may never be able to parlay their way to being more than penny-ante brokers. But others have learned how to intimidate people with words, or throw their weight around by virtue of their deftly acquired positions. Still others may appear to agree with, or at least not to vehemently disagree with their opponents in public, but they muster their forces in the background to wage war when the time is more opportune. In all cases, however, the opinionated power broker is largely unteachable and virtually implacable.

*Goals:* An opinionated person with a network of pliable friends is potentially dangerous; but clearly defined goals turn the powder keg into a ball of fire. The power broker has goals to reach and the means to reach them. The goal may be to get a pet project done; it may be to get rid of the youth minister; it may be to build a playground, or establish a daycare, or get rid of the daycare. It may be to see that the deacons are in charge of buildings and grounds, or to get a sign for the church, or to keep the preacher from getting a sign for the church. It may be to force the use of certain materials in the Sunday School, or to convince the congregation not to change hymn books. Ultimately, the goal may be to rid the church of the ineffective pastor (identified by his not cooperating with the power broker) and to get a new one (who will).

But really the ultimate goal of the power broker is to enhance his or her own power. For power brokers, for all they may say about how they have the good of the church in mind, mostly have themselves in mind. They enjoy being in control: they need to be in control. And they have learned how to get what they want.

*Case Study 10*
Miles Massey (not his real name) served as pastor of the

TSR Church in an urban area. He joined a staff consisting of a secretary and an older minister of music, who shortly retired.

It didn't take Miles long to discover that there were two very powerful people in the church. One was John Best (not his real name), a retired gentlemen who was fairly wealthy as the result of years of good business ventures. But he had also spent all his adult life in the TSR Church, much of it as the director of the Sunday School. His work in the church was one of the major reasons it had prospered for many years. Mr. Best was powerful because of his tireless work and his proven wisdom. What he thought ought to take place in the church usually did, but only because those in leadership saw the intrinsic wisdom in his thoughts. Benevolent to the bone, Best had never abused his enormous influence.

The second very powerful person was Tom Summer (not his real name, either). Tom was a generation younger than Best, and like him had been in the TSR church all his adult life. In fact, the Summer and Best families were very close, and Summer regarded Best as his mentor and model.

Unfortunately for the church, Summer's influence, also significant, was not as benevolent. Usually it was; but Summer was self-seeking and carnal. All it took for those qualities to come out was for something about which he was opinionated to go against him.

Pastor Massey unwittingly provided Summer with the necessary provocation. After the retirement of the aging music minister, Summer was one of five members elected to find the replacement. Apparently, he had been waiting for this moment to arrive, for with his able guidance the committee found a candidate in about six weeks. They went rapidly and perfunctorily through the steps to present the candidate to the church, including arranging with the pastor for the two to meet and spend some time together.

Massey and the candidate did meet and talk, and while Pastor Massey couldn't lay his finger on anything major that seemed to be problematic, he had the feeling from how rapidly the search was conducted that he was being set up somehow. Massey wrote later that he never said anything to committee members or anyone else about his feelings, but he wondered if the candidate himself had sensed his uneasiness.

At any rate, Massey told Summer and the other committee members he believed he could work with the candidate successfully if he were called. Tom Summer on behalf of the committee presented the man to the church and the church called him. However, one week before he was supposed to come on the field, he called to say he had changed his mind. Much later, Massey recalls, he learned that the candidate had been a close friend of Summer's, and had told him he felt the pastor didn't like him.

Pastor Massey took charge of things and reconvened the committee himself. After several meetings he presented the committee with a name to consider. The person he recommended was a friend in ministry. The committee did not generate any other candidates on its own, and eventually it recommended the pastor's friend. The church called him, and he came.

Summer was not the same from that time. He was a deacon, and within a year he maneuvered within the body to have himself elected vice-chairman. The vice-chairman always moved up to chairman after a year. After waiting patiently, he became chairman. At his second meeting as chairman he called an executive session and requested that the pastor leave the meeting. When the deacons met the next month, they had an uneasy and serious discussion with the pastor about the general state of the church and the advisability of his looking for someplace else to go.

While the meeting would never have happened if all had been well in Zion, the fact is that things had not been well under the previous pastor either, and in fact had declined sharply. Under Massey's leadership the church had stopped the downward snowball and was maintaining its own. The church had a typical mix of discouragement and victory, and much reason for optimism. But Summer had used every contact he had, magnified every complaint he had heard, called in every favor he was owed, and cast enough doubt and fear into deacons' and other people's minds to be successful in coercing the pastor to leave.

Massey left within three months after being courted by a church in another state. But he wrote later that he caved when he should have stood firm. He admitted that his relative youth contributed to his being intimidated by the power broker and his grumbling followers.

*Case Study 11*

The QPO Church of a western city was being swallowed by a metroplex and surrounded by new apartments and condominiums. Within a period of just a few years, most homeowners in the church's neighborhood had sold property to developers for a hefty profit and had moved. Sellers who were QPO members left the church as well. Now counting fifty people in attendance any given Sunday, QPO Church was struggling and filled with gloom. New pastor Darrell Propst (naturally, not his real name) came with the conviction that the church needed to reclaim what members it could and to reach the new neighbors somehow. He didn't succeed. The decline was permanent, the members were wistful and lethargic, the average age was sixty, and the pastor's plan simply didn't work. After a year or so, he was very discouraged.

Enter Carl Johns. Carl was the age of most of the members, and had been at the church only a short time. But Carl was a forceful person, a fast talking debater who had been a teacher and knew how to lead. Carl's background was uncertain, but he was clearly knowledgeable about the Bible, and frequently engaged the pastor and others in discussions about theological issues. Sometimes his points dealt with minutia, but he always seemed to be advancing some as yet undisclosed agenda.

Eventually, he was asked to teach a class. Before he accepted, he asked the pastor if it was okay with him. Not certain why it wouldn't be, the pastor gave his blessing. Before long, the reason became evident. Carl had come out of a strong, Calvinist background, and was on a personal mission to convert churches to Calvinist theology wherever he went. Somehow, between the unfamiliarity of both the members and the pastor with the vocabulary and key concepts of Calvinism, no one realized prior to this time what Carl's motives were. Within a short time, this gifted teacher had class members eating out of his hand. The class was mesmerized by the fascinating discussions and lectures, but it became totally inactive in outreach.

One of those class members was Richard, a forty-ish man, regarded as the next patriarch of the church, if it lasted long enough to have one. Carl convinced Richard, who had more clout with all the members, that the pastor was not of the right theological ilk for the struggling church. Richard believed Carl Johns, and in turn put pressure on the pastor, not on theological grounds—which he didn't really understand—but on the basis of the church's malaise.

It turns out that the pastor, without knowing it, tended toward fairly strong Calvinism himself. But Carl Johns apparently didn't think it was strong enough. In any event, the merits of Calvinism are irrelevant to this case: the problem in the QPO church was that it was ripe for manipulation by a strong leader, and one appeared on cue. A pastor was hurt in the process, and in the aftermath the church was hurt as well. Sidetracked from its need of outreach, the church closed its doors within two years.

In the previous case studies, principally one person

instigated maneuvers against the pastor with the support of a network of family and friends, or with the help of pliable recruits. These individuals succeeded in reaching their goals, defeating their pastors and contributing to the churches' partial or total destruction.

## The Wake They Leave Behind

Power brokers have inspired tomes of unpublished book material from the pens of their former pastors and not a few fellow church members. Some of the stories in this book came from church members, not pastors.

Many a person disgusted and exasperated by power politics in his or her church has left that church when his ousted pastor did. Unfortunately, the exodus of such members merely strengthens the broker's power by reducing the size of his opposition. But what can the disappointed member do? If he does not believe himself influential enough to make a difference, he has only three basic options: stand by and watch, and then get over it, pretending to forget; join in the fray and be marked as an opponent ever after; or leave, and try to find a church where at least at present no conflict is ongoing.

What members fleeing conflict leave behind is a bad memory. But what power brokers leave behind is a trail of confusion and division. It is a trail where churches are sidetracked by what are frequently peripheral issues. It is a trail of infighting, distrust, and cynicism, a trail littered with alienated brethren, fragmented fellowship, and wounded babes in Christ.

Lamentably, few power brokers ever own up to the carnage they cause. Most of them go on believing that the church just had a bad pastor, or a string of them. It may have, but more likely the culprit is the power broker. And he is apt to strike again and again, wherever he goes, until and unless he is confronted and changed.

Christ designed his church to function effectively under the leadership of the persons he gifted and sent to them. Even where churches operate in a framework of congregational government, their polity is not meant to be a tacit invitation to members to acquire controlling power through shrewd politics. The church that has too many chiefs usually finds itself having a constant war party, and may eventually find itself in a burial mound.

Many people vying for power is a recipe for division that cooks into disabling trouble for churches and pastors. But in other ways as well, churches disable their own leaders. Various church activity winds up hamstringing the lead sheep.

# 8

## Hamstringing the Lead Sheep

**Pharaoh gave this order to the slave drivers and foremen in charge of the people: "You are no longer to supply the people with straw for making bricks; let them go and gather their own straw. But require them to make the same number of bricks as before; don't reduce the quota."**
**Exodus 5:7-8 NIV**

The ancient practice of hamstringing involved cutting the hamstring of an enemy's horse, the great tendon on the back of the hock, corresponding to the human ankle on a horse's back leg. Obviously, this action rendered the horse lame, and forced the enemy to destroy it. When an army hamstrung its enemy's horses, it both disabled and humiliated that army's cavalry.

*A church, by organizational strategy or by tradition, can hamstring its pastor, having the effect of both disabling and humiliating him, as well as the church he is trying to serve.*

## Official Policies

One would certainly think it would be counterproductive to call a pastor and yet to have official policies that make it difficult for him to carry out his duties. Yet, that is exactly what some church policies do. Whether or not they are designed to have a negative impact on the pastor in his work, the effect is the same:

- The pastor is expected to lead the church. Yet as we have discussed at length elsewhere in this book, the pastor is often prohibited by express, constitutional or bylaw provisions, from making the decisions that may be essential in order to accomplish that leadership. Members sometimes defend these provisions by saying that the people need to be involved in making the decisions or else they won't go along with what is decided. Or members may actually say their constitution is framed in this way to prevent a pastor from becoming a dictator.
  Such rationalizations amount to official justification of stubbornness at best, and rank cynicism and distrust at worst. While pastors don't need executive authority over every matter in a church (and most wouldn't even want it), they cannot function as leaders if they have essentially none.
- In the typical church the pastor is to be the head the staff. But somehow he is to accomplish this task without being able to hire or fire staff, or without being

able to supervise them in any meaningful way, as we have discussed elsewhere. Policies concerning staff supervision vary widely, of course, and some pastors are not subject to the same limitations as others.

- Church constitutions frequently say that the pastor is to "work with the deacons." This hazy description sounds biblical, but it may actually be code language for "cooperate with the deacons." The biblical model indicates that pastors should have strong input in the appointment of deacons, and that deacons should assist the pastor. But more often than not these days church constitutions specifically provide for a manner of deacon selection that leaves the pastor out entirely, or involves him in a peripheral way only. Very few churches accord the pastor the authority to approve or disapprove the nomination of a deacon. Yet pastors know that the choice of some men is inimical to their ministries, and in some cases it was malignantly intended to be. Furthermore, in vast numbers of churches the deacons function on their own quite apart from the genuine leadership of the pastor. It is debatable whether or not the internal organization of deacons is ultimately beneficial to the church, or whether it implies from the very outset the possibility of there being two sets of agenda, one the pastor's and one the deacons'.
- The pastor is also usually commissioned to "give general direction" to the church. But another group may actually have this task, such as deacons or a church council. The pastor's role in giving general direction

may indeed be extremely general, amounting to little more than making suggestions in front of another official body. As with other problems, this difficulty may be critical in one church and virtually absent from another. But any pastor who has encountered it has felt hamstrung as the lead sheep.

## Traditional Approaches

Since the time of Jesus and long before, tradition has been a potential source of behavior antithetical to God's revealed standards. Jesus lambasted tradition in saying that the Pharisees had made the commitment of significant sums of money to God such a sacrosanct practice that they thought it justified failing to support their aging parents. Jesus said, "You nullify the word of God for the sake of your tradition" (Mat.15:6 NIV). Of other practices dearly held by Pharisees and teachers of the law Jesus said, "You have let go of the commands of God and are holding on to the traditions of men," and then added, "And you do many things like that" (Mk.7:8,13 NIV).

Traditions vary with the church, but certainly one common theme found almost everywhere is the body of tradition that virtually controls the order and content of worship. Pastors, conscious of their responsibility to lead worship, may feel it necessary to revise the typical approach to worship:

- The pastor may want to introduce new elements into the

worship time, or to delete or reduce elements that conflict with the purpose of worship or unnecessarily lengthen the worship time. For instance, they may want to shorten announcements, or eliminate them altogether, or move them to the end of the service. Or they may want to abbreviate or redesign the way that visitors are recognized or welcomed.
- The pastor may want to reorder events, not just to shake things up, but to communicate some solid theological principle, such as placing the offering at the end of the service to emphasize that it is a response to the preached message or the other content of the worship hour. Or they may prefer to locate an invitation time someplace else.
- The pastor may feel that the imposition of an hour's limit on the length of the service is detrimental to the concept of the Holy Spirit's expected moving. He may approach a solution by extending the service in an open-ended manner, or planning an additional time increment, as when multiple worship services must begin and end at a specific hour.

But let the pastor—even the pastor and the staff together—make these decisions because they are taking seriously their role as the leaders of worship, and they will generally find out very quickly how little they actually lead. Tradition tends to be sacred, and the objections raised to changes instigated by the pastor or other staff are usually expressed as violating what the church has always done, rather than being debated on the basis of any theological or even practical reasons.

## Case Study 13

In one church the pastor moved announcements from ten minutes into the church service to the five minutes before worship began. Choir members soon passed around disgruntled reports. When word eventually reached the staff, the reason given was that the choir didn't enter until after the announcements were over. However, the plan had called for the minister of music to give the same announcements in the choir room before the service. There was no substance to the complaint. The change simply wasn't traditional.

In the same church, the pastor and staff noted how announcements frequently took upwards of ten minutes, and frequently contained reminders of items already published in the church newsletter or in the bulletin already in the hands of everyone attending worship that day. Deciding that reading information everyone could read for himself was repetitious and perhaps even insulting, the staff agreed to repeat only the most important information, such as promoting a seasonal offering or reminding the congregation of unusual schedule alterations or highly special events. And they concentrated on things that affected the whole church, rather than small groups. In addition, they requested that all information on group activities be submitted to the church office by a certain time each week, and they were careful to publicize these items in the newsletter and/or bulletin.

On Sundays, however, the staff received multiple notes under their doors or left on their desks about events that "needed" to be announced but had not been submitted in time to be published. Also frequently, people came up to the pastor or minister of youth or music five minutes before the service, with just one more promotional item. When the announcement time didn't include all these items, or when the item contained material already in the bulletin and thus was not repeated verbally by the staff in worship, grumbling ensued. No amount of education changed the traditional mind-set.

The pastor recounts that he explained to a certain lady in the church (one more time) the rational for not repeating items already printed in front of them, and assured her that whoever did the announcements would continue to encourage everyone to note the announcements in the bulletin. This church member explained her devotion to the traditional, extended announcement time by saying, "But people don't read the bulletin. If we don't announce it, they won't know about it."

Sometimes, you just can't win.

*Case Study 14*

Another minister, after a year on the field in a large, regional church, began instituting changes in the worship service as a natural outgrowth of his theology and his vision for the church. Various elements were switched around, and a time of fellowship and greeting was added.

Partly as a consequence, as well as because the new minister preached a bit longer on average, the service was extended by around fifteen minutes, though it still dismissed before noon because of its starting time.

The wheels of traditional power-groups began turning. Soon they began to put pressure on the pastor to "go back to the way things were." At last report he hadn't; but the issue was far from settled.

The "issue" is not whether or not people agree with the reason for a particular change: the issue is whether or not the pastor is going to be allowed to lead the church in worship. If he is not, then a church should simply elect a worship committee to devise the worship order, and prospective pastors should be fully advised of this fact. Perhaps if a great many churches have to go through two or three times the usual number of pastoral candidates before they find one who will go along with their plan, the point will become clear. Who is leading whom?

In a way, a pastor's encountering such resistance from tradition is a predictable, routine frustration, not the stuff of major crisis. But pastors have been pressured to resign for just such contributing reasons. The resistance of tradition is just one more way a church steeped in its own habits manages to hamstring the lead sheep.

### Typical Behavior

Certain other behavior patterns work against the

pastor's ministry or effectiveness that don't fall neatly into either the category of policy or tradition. Rather they seem simply to be *typical behavior*. These are the things people do out of human nature, and upon which most preaching, teaching, counseling or chiding has little effect.

- The pastor is expected to get to know the members. But many pastors these days in particular have come to realize that in this grand task they wind up taking almost all the initiative. Like teenage girls in the fifties, members sit at home waiting for a call. These members never make the first move to make friends with the pastor. They don't invite him to dinner or out to lunch. They don't come by the office just to introduce themselves. They wait for the pastor to make the first move, and every move thereafter. If just some of them would initiate the relationship, they would help pastors immensely.

  Many observers of church history and culture have noted that whereas in the past it was customary for the new pastor to receive more invitations than he could handle to have dinner in a member family's home or to go to a certain event with them, nowadays he may hear from fewer families than he could count on one hand, or none at all. The cultural change has everything to do with the activity level of the typical family, and with the failure of certain habits of courtesy to be transmitted from one generation to another. Whatever the cause, this cultural change has added significantly to the burden placed on the pastor to make all the moves toward friendship. There are 300, or 500, or 2,000 members, and one pastor. It would seem reasonable if they wanted a date, some of them would call him, instead of sitting at home by the phone.

- The pastor is supposed to lead the church in prayer. One way churches have attempted to teach, encourage and practice prayer in the past is by having a midweek prayer meeting. But attendance at prayer meeting is universally low, owing in part to its very nature as an event appealing to the more spiritually mature or hungry, whose number in any church is always far fewer than the total or even the active membership. But another obstacle to prayer meeting is the typical behavior of various organizational leaders in scheduling their own meetings for the same hour the pastor is trying to gather the church together to talk with God.

Occasionally, even the other staff members (notably youth leaders) plan things to coincide with prayer meeting. But women's missionary groups, men's groups, and various church committees are frequently the culprits. A committee chairman not in the habit of going to prayer meeting may schedule his meeting for the same hour figuring that it doesn't make any difference for him. Tragically, none of his committee members may care either.

The pastor who tries to get his church to reserve the midweek hour for prayer meeting alone is trying to do two things: keep people from having to make a choice between activities; and encourage people to be present for a vital time in the life of the church. It's part of what the church called him to do. But typical activity works against him.

- The pastor is also expected to visit the sick. Most pastors make a valiant try to meet this obligation, and many preachers find it rewarding to be with someone who feels acutely his or her need and is readily open to spiritual encouragement. But a church's typical behavior again interferes.

For every dear lady who cannot seem to stop calling the pastor about her little woes, there are ten other men or women who will not inform the pastor or church office about sickness, hospitalization, injury or surgery. One of these ten really doesn't feel the need of a pastoral visit, even if he happens to be in the hospital. This rare person really doesn't expect the pastor to come see him because he doesn't feel the need of ministry, and that's why he doesn't tell him anything.

But with the other nine it's a different story. They don't call, but it's not because they don't expect the preacher to call them or come see them. They do expect it. They expect that someone they told casually, with no message to tell the pastor, will tell someone else who will tell someone else who will tell the pastor. Or worse, they expect the pastor to find out on his own, through means unknown—osmosis? ESP? a word of knowledge from the Lord?

Like resistance to changes in the worship service, the typical behavior of church members in resisting the leadership of the pastor in prayer, visiting the sick or getting to know the membership could be thought of as just one more routine frustration that every pastor deals with. But the sad thing is that such skirmishes or resistance movements within the church have come to be thought of as routine. For no matter how universal they may be, they are still ways in which church members hamstring the lead sheep and work against his ministry and leadership.

In the long run, it is they who are hurt more than he. It is their church that does not grow spiritually as it could, that does not grow numerically as it might, or that even declines and dies, because it called a man to lead but then did not follow.

A church may hamstring its pastor because of its underlying distrust. But even more curious than what churches *don't* want their pastors to do is what they *do* want them to do, which may in fact be beyond their ability. We turn now to see how churches may want their pastors to fill shoes they don't fit.

# 9

# Promulgating a Theology of Exaltation

**Sirs, why do ye these things? We also are men of like passions with you.**
**Acts 14:15**

Such amazing things occurred in the apostles' ministries that occasionally people mistook them for gods. The citizens of Lystra exalted Paul and Barnabas to the positions of Mercury and Jupiter before Paul could straighten them out by telling them loudly, "We're men just like you!"

With a sense of trepidation, a related subject should be broached at this point. Churches in general appear to have promulgated a theology of exaltation with regard to the role of their pastors. This theology is not expressly stated, but rather implied.

> *Some church members have unwittingly conferred on their pastors a ministry role that can be fulfilled by God alone.*

Obviously, a statement like that demands explanation, and for two reasons:

- Many Christians do not readily recognize any sense in which they have too highly exalted their pastors.
- The evidence of deep and widespread rebellion in churches—on which this book has focused in detail—seems to suggest the opposite idea, that pastors are respected *too little*.

Obviously, the church whose members feel free to displace their pastor for one of a host of unbiblical reasons does not appear to be elevating the pastor or exalting his role. On the surface, quite the opposite appears to be the case. Curiously, however, in many churches the pastor is held in low regard as a decision-making leader, but held to an extremely high standard with regard to inspiring people or solving their myriad problems. While the church may hamstring its pastor in his divine calling to lead, it may prod and spur him to perform spiritual duties for which he is not and never could be equipped.

Bluntly put, some church members expect the pastor to be the spiritual father of the entire congregation, the personal shepherd of each Christian, and the comforting presence in every life and family—all of which cast the pastor in the role of the triune God.

Hardly any Christian would ever say that his pastor *should* be the next thing to God to his church. Nor would any self-respecting or God-respecting pastor suggest it, either. But the evidence of many church members' behavior suggests that their expectations of their pastor are tantamount to exalting him to a position rightfully occupied by the Lord only. Some people verbalize the idea that the pastor is "only human," but in practice they expect superhuman performance.

### Jesus Christ is Our True Shepherd

A truth taught by the scriptures but not fully realized by most believers is that their church's pastor is not their personal, true shepherd: *only Christ the Lord is.*

### The Lord is my shepherd…(Ps.23:1)

Jesus declared himself the one who shepherds the sheep. In John 10:11-16 he described himself as the "good shepherd" by virtue of his very being, and defined his role as giving his life for the sheep, caring for the sheep, protecting his sheep, knowing his sheep, and bringing or leading his sheep. His language echoes the description of David's expectation of "The Lord" in Psalm 23:

- **He *maketh* me to lie down in green pastures…**
- **He *leadeth* me beside the still waters…**
- **He *restoreth* my soul…**
- **He *leadeth* me in the paths of righteousness…**

Others ministries mentioned in Psalm 23 can be performed sufficiently only by the Lord himself:

- **Thou art *with* me…**

- **Thy rod and thy staff they *comfort* me...**
- **Thou preparest a *table* before me...**
- **Thou *anointest* my head with oil...**

These are the ministries of continual presence, divine comfort, feeding of the soul, and spiritual cleansing and empowerment. Only the Lord can perform these things. In his relationship to Christians as Father, Son and Spirit, God himself shepherds us.

In what way, then, do Christians occasionally or frequently put their pastors in shoes that only the Lord should fill?

*Only the pastor will do*

Many a church flirts with exalting its pastor to a role reserved to the Lord when the widespread attitude is that when a need of ministry arises, only the pastor will do to meet it. In many a church of small to medium size in particular, when a member is sick or hospitalized it may be *nice* to have a deacon or Sunday School teacher visit or call, but it's *necessary* for the pastor to do so. Until he has, the required ministry is not considered to have been performed. Even in churches having an associate pastor, many members regard the visit of such ministers as secondary or temporary, and expect the head pastor to tend to them himself eventually.

Most pastors would not dream of declining to visit a home where there has been a death. But as the severity of need declines, there comes a point, especially in larger churches, at which the pastor would spend much of every day's labor just calling or visiting everyone with a real or perceived need. And for every need, no matter how minor, that he may try to meet, someone will always complain later that he or she was sick and the pastor never called.

As pointed out earlier, nearly every pastor has had the criticism get back to him that someone was out of church two Sundays and he didn't notice that person's absence or call or come by. Once a church exceeds several dozen members, most pastors find it humanly impossible to look at a congregation from the platform and immediately be aware of who is and is not present. This is exactly the point: it is not *humanly* possible. It is only *divinely* possible. Only God can do it.

Most churches expect their pastor, not some other person, to visit all church members once or twice per year (if not more), to visit all shut-ins and nursing home residents several additional times per year, to visit all hospitalized members every day or every other day, to visit in the homes of the bereaved several times around the time of a death, and to make other visits occasioned by sickness, injury, spiritual trouble or family discord or other needs. In a church of 200 members, this expectation would not be burdensome on average.

But in a church of only 500 members, a pastor would have to visit three hours per day, four days a week, assuming he is "granted" the privilege of reserving one work day for uninterrupted study and prayer. And in a church of 1,000 members, if the pastor alone were expected to make all the needed visits, he would have to spend six hours a day out in the neighborhoods and in the hospitals and nursing homes.

When will the pastor spend those 20 hours every seminary recommends that he spend on each of the two sermons he preaches? Where will he find the additional 5-10 hours needed to prepare a Bible study or other materials for Wednesday nights? How will he fit in the daily hours needed to take care of office administration, planning, and staff communication and guidance? Will there be time left for associational activities or for counseling? Will he be able to attend every class party or social, go on every youth trip, or go with the senior adults every time they sally forth to the mountains or the beach?

All these and many more duties the typical pastor is expected to perform add up to about a sixty-five hour work week including Sunday duties. And none of the foregoing description even mentioned the pastor's need to engage in evangelistic visitation and soul-winning! In a church of average size, the burden of being "the only one who will do" casts the pastor in a role it is not *humanly* possible to perform. Again, this is exactly the point: The pastor is a human being, not God.

The solution to the pastor's being expected to perform all these duties in too little time is not that somehow the Lord should be the Shepherd and perform these ministries without the pastor or anyone else making visits or touching lives. It is rather for other staff members, deacons and other persons to share the load in a significant way. This will require two things to take place:

- Church members must realize that the Lord by his Spirit is the true Shepherd of the sheep.
- Deacons and others must realize that they, too, can and must become the ministers of the presence of God in the lives of others, and the conduits by whom the Great Shepherd touches his sheep.

*Depending on the pastor for inspiration*

Members often expect the pastor not only to be a ubiquitous presence in the community when he's not in the pulpit, but also to be a superhuman presence when he is. While many church members would balk at the suggestion that they expect the divine from a human being, in fact the expectations of many people boil down to just that.

- They do little preparation for the worship hour themselves, and then expect the events of worship, as planned by the pastor, to generate an exciting worship experience in their lives.
- They expect the sermon to touch every life, meet every need, inspire the lethargic, invigorate the lifeless, and illuminate those in the dark.
- They expect God to convict the sinner, save the lost, and fill the saved in the worship service, and when it doesn't happen, it must be the preacher's fault.

Not only church members but preachers themselves hold

some of these expectations of themselves, and feel guilty when a worship service seems to fall flat, or when weeks and weeks go by with no decisions, either by the lost or the saved. Preachers in general take very seriously their responsibility to be mouthpieces for the word of God, and their role as both ministers of love and bearers of the gospel. But sometimes they blame themselves for dead bodies in the pews when it is no fault of their own. Yet the dead rise up from their pews and frequently hold the pastor responsible for the entire process of worship and their experience of spiritual life and excitement.

No suggestion is being made that church members consciously put the pastor on a pedestal they *know* only God can occupy, and even less that pastors themselves *think* they are God. What is being said is only that some *unwittingly* define the role of the pastor as including responsibilities that only the Lord himself can fulfill.

This too-high expectation is only exacerbated by the fact that most worship attenders today do not prepare for worship at home or even when they arrive at church. They may do nothing at all at home during the week or on Saturday night, or even early Sunday, to prepare their hearts for a time of worship with the church. Even after entering the place of worship, they may spend the last few minutes before the service talking with people around them—often loudly—or looking around at what everyone is wearing, or sorting through purses and other belongings. Pre-service instrumental music is routinely ignored. Groups of teens may wander across the front of the auditorium and elsewhere, stopping in little clusters for conversation, sometimes boisterous.

Many worship bulletins used to encourage attenders to meditate quietly upon entering the worship room, but few church members observe this etiquette anymore, much less regard it as a spiritual obligation.

*Case Study 15*

A member of a large church in South Carolina recounted how he sat weekly near the front of the auditorium and spent pre-service time praying, his eyes closed and head bowed or in his hands. Nearly every week someone would enter from the front of the room, pass where he was seated and jostle or poke him, some just to say, "Hi!" but some to tell him to "wake up!" He said he wondered if it even occurred to any of them that he might actually be praying in church. One Sunday he moved from the front to the back row, and spent the pre-service moments praying, his Bible open on his lap. With three minutes to go before the service began, someone shook him and said loudly, "If you hurry you can just make it into the choir!"

Inspiring stories are told about churches where groups of people gather near the sanctuary to pray for the service, or where a spirit of holiness descends upon the gathered worshipers in the auditorium. But for every one of those accounts one could easily tally many, many more where no sense of impending worship could be felt prior to the service. Yet when the hour begins, many church members expect the events, rhythm, sounds, and words of the service to create a worship experience. If the service does not accomplish this expectation, one person usually absorbs the blame: the pastor.

*The mediator for the only mediator*

Ultimately, expectations by some Christians of their pastors rise to the dangerous level of making him responsible for their own spiritual lives and growth. While the pastor's role certainly is to preach the word and feed the flock spiritually, at some point the sheep must reasonably take responsibility for themselves. If horses can be led to water but not made to drink, then Christians—certainly those who have been believers for a while—become responsible for their own spiritual walks. The pastor/preacher cannot *humanly* address every issue affecting every life of every church member or visitor and speak to all these needs as they are occurring.

The only one who can minister to these needs is Jesus Christ. While the lost need the preacher or some concerned Christian to be their means of learning the saving truth of the gospel, every Christian is charged with the responsibility of his or her own spiritual growth. The pastor cannot be responsible for the personal discipleship and fruitfulness of every member of the church. It is not *humanly* possible, no matter how devoted he may be. Yet many of the disappointments and disillusionments of members with their pastors stem from the underlying assumption on their part that if he had just been a better pastor, either they or someone else would have been more inspired, more satisfied, or less sinful, or would not have left the church.

All these descriptions of members' frequent expectations stress how some things simply are not *humanly* possible. They are illustrations of the exaltation of the pastor to a role that only deity can fulfill.

It is precisely because of this exaltation of the pastor to a ministry only Christ can perform, that church members expect too much of the pastor. They expect more of him in this kind of ministry than is possible for him to perform, no matter how many visits he might make or how much time he might spend or how close he might get to any particular person. And because he cannot perform this ministry, he "fails," and is then the focus of the church member's disappointment. There is no way for him to avoid disappointing people who see him as the provider of their spiritual growth, excitement, enthusiasm for church, reality in worship, or any other thing only God can do in a Christian's life. Until people stop expecting such things of the pastor, they will continue to be disillusioned, and pastors will continue to be displaced for disappointing them.

### Getting Our Eyes Off Man

All this discussion of what is or is not too much expectation of the pastor is not simply the complaint of this writer or of various overworked pastors. It is founded in scriptures such as Psalm 23:1, previously mentioned, and in other passages where the Bible emphasizes the vital concept that the eyes of God's people must be on God, not on man.

Psalm 23:1 focuses on the shepherd, which ultimately we know to be Jesus Christ, who identified himself in that role. Pastors are *under*-shepherds, merely assistants to the Chief Shepherd.

If the scriptures admonish us not to exalt human beings to the place only the Son of God should occupy, do they also warn us about usurping the roles of the Father and the Spirit? Indeed they do!

- **The Father** - Jesus told his disciples specifically, "Call no man your father upon earth; for one is your Father, which is in heaven." Clearly he was speaking of titles given to those in spiritual leadership (not fathers of families), since in the same context he warned against referring to the same people as "rabbi." It is surprising that such plain language has been ignored by so many who claim the Christian faith.
- **The Spirit** - The apostle John wrote in 1 John 2:27, "the anointing which ye have received of him abideth in you, and ye need not that any *man* teach you: but as the same anointing teacheth you of all things, and is truth, and is no lie, and even as it hath taught you, ye shall abide in *him*" (italics ours). The meaning is obvious: While the Lord calls pastors, teachers, apostles, prophets, and

evangelists and places elders in his church to guide and teach, *ultimately* there is only one teacher, the Holy Spirit of the Lord.

We are always to be mindful that no one can take the place of the Spirit in our lives. We must never make any person, whether pastor, Sunday School teacher, parent or spouse, or radio teacher or TV preacher or anyone else, so important to our personal spiritual lives that he displaces the Spirit of God. Not only is that too heavy a burden for any human being, but it is the epitome of idolatry for the one doing it.

## Who is Your Pastor, Anyway?

A probing question every church member should ask is, "Who is my pastor, anyway?" Many people are fond of referring to their church's leader as "my pastor." But doesn't Psalm 23:1 say that "the Lord is my shepherd?" Since *pastor* and *shepherd* are the same word in Hebrew and the same word in Greek, which one is my pastor: the preacher, or Christ the Lord?

Perhaps there is no actual dilemma: Christ is the shepherd and the pastor is the under-shepherd. But the term *undershepherd* does not appear in the Bible. The Greek word for shepherd is used for a church's pastor as well as for Jesus Christ. We use the term "under-shepherd" to designate the church's pastor in order to distinguish the human being who wears that title in his limited role from the divine being who bears it supremely. The distinction between Christ's role as the Shepherd and the pastor's role as a shepherd must be inferred from all scripture references to their respective ministries.

The suggestion of Psalm 23:1 is that the role of *personal* shepherd, *personal* guide, *personal* protector of *each* sheep is one that belongs to Jesus Christ himself, and no other. A church's pastor, on the other hand, appears to be a shepherd to the *corporate* church more than to its individuals. Every reference in the New Testament to elders in their pastoral role (and there are only a few) is set in a context of a *corporate* role, not a *personal* one.

Caution, now! This is not to suggest that the ministry of a church's pastor is not personal. It is to clarify the vital point taught in scripture that the Lord Jesus is the personal shepherd of each of his sheep, and that no human being can substitute for him. Neither should a church expect its pastor to try.

*Pastors as an illustration*

The experience of pastors themselves illustrates the truth of this scriptural teaching. Consider the question: who is the pastor's pastor? If Christians are justified in considering the church pastor their *personal* pastor, and if, as is only reasonable, every Christian should have a shepherd, then do pastors simply get left out? Or have they "arrived" in the faith, such that they do not need a pastor as other people do?

In connectional churches pastors are on a lower level of the ecclesiastical hierarchy. Above them are bishops or other persons who head up higher levels of the church's structure. In such churches—typified by the Episcopal or Roman Catholic bodies—the local pastor may reasonably consider his immediate superior to be his pastor. Even so, the relationship is not the same as with a congregant and his or her church pastor.

For the vast number of pastors who serve congregational churches, there is no one "above" them in the church structure. The pastor of a congregational church is the highest human, spiritual authority in those denominations. Do these pastors have no pastors?

Many Southern Baptist pastors consider their associational directors of missions their pastors, and regularly confide in them and seek their counsel. And some men in leadership positions in conventions or denominational offices of various churches style themselves as pastors to the larger body of their churches in a region or state. But if some pastors find for themselves someone to lend counsel or impart wisdom, it doesn't mean this person is their pastor in any official sense. It only means these pastors do what any and *every* Christian should do and may do freely, irrespective of the *position* held by the one whose help they seek.

The question remains: who is the pastor's pastor—not his good friend or his trusted advisor or his spiritual confidant, but his official pastor? In congregational churches at least, he has no pastor.

But in fact, he does. "The Lord is my shepherd—I shall not want." The Lord is the pastor's pastor, his shepherd.

But in fact, the Lord is every Christian's shepherd, every Christian's personal pastor, in a vastly more important way than any earthly pastor can ever function.

If the pastor himself finds his own true pastor in the Lord Jesus, he demonstrates the validity of this scriptural truth for all church members. Whatever role the pastor may play in the lives of individual church members in addition to his clear role as leader of the corporate flock, the individual role must never become so important to a member Christian—no matter how needy—as to eclipse his responsibility to seek the Lord himself as his Shepherd.

When church members lay on their pastor the impossible duty of being a substitute teacher for the Holy Spirit, or a stand-in for the Great Shepherd, they make trouble for that pastor, and set themselves up for disillusionment. Where such expectations are widespread and ingrained, a church is destined to experience trouble.

The Lord will continue to call pastors to lead his churches, to repeat his words, to articulate his truth, and to communicate by their physical presence in ministry the invisible but very real presence of Christ. But Christ himself is every believer's true pastor, and church members must guard themselves against expecting the church's pastor to do for them spiritually what only the Lord Jesus Christ himself can.

# 10

# Chronic Vexations

**Obey your leaders and submit to their authority. They keep watch over you as men who must give an account. Obey them so that their work will be a joy, not a burden, for that would be of no advantage to you.**
**Hebrews 13:17 NIV**

Curiously, some churches as a whole seem intent on keeping their pastors in a state of stress and distress. While most employers in the world count employee happiness a valuable asset to business, many churches do not live by the same philosophy. These churches' members have not stopped to think of how their typical behavior affects the pastors they have called to lead them in the most important business on earth: knowing Christ and making him known.

*Many chronic behavior patterns in churches rob pastors of joy, dull their enthusiasm for ministry, and consequently have a reciprocal effect on the church's spiritual health.*

In many automobile accidents there is one primary cause but several contributing causes. With the coming of cell phones, and particularly the smart phone, it has become abundantly evident that these conveniences can be blamed for many accidents. Various states have passed laws banning the use of cell phones while driving, due to the distraction they produce. However, it isn't just sending text messages or doing other things that require looking at the phone's screen; it's also the regular phone conversation that deserves some blame. There is no end to anecdotal evidence from other drivers who were, or were nearly, hit by cars whose drivers were staring blankly around because their minds' eyes were conjuring up images of the persons they were talking to.

Similarly, church turmoil and pastoral exoduses are usually due directly to one or two main causes; however, quite often other contributing causes can be identified as well. Various behaviors by church members function in a contributory way to the frustration, disappointment, discouragement, or even anger of pastors, and thus engender an unhealthy relationship with their churches, and possibly help lead to the end of the relationship altogether.

## Withheld Feedback

A pastor standing at the front door of the church as people leave the Sunday service is one of the quintessential images of Christian ministry. In those brief encounters at the church's doors, pastors hear repeatedly all possible variations on the words, "wonderful sermon." Overwhelmingly, the reports are glowing, positive, and appreciative.

There are some confusing exceptions. One woman who lived in something of a perpetual fog left the service one morning and told her pastor that she really enjoyed all his sermons. She added, "Every one is better than the next."

Another lady, impressed by her pastor's delivery of a sermon entirely in verse, exited with these words: "That was wonderful, and very interesting. Where did you get that sermon? Did you write it yourself or did you get it out of a book?" Did she mean it was good enough to have come from a famous author, or that she assumed her pastor was incapable of producing what he did?

Other remarks are not the least bit vague, and are delightfully genuine. For the most part, however, the tradition of greeting the pastor on the way out of the worship hour provides a convenient opportunity to express polite appreciation without the necessity of thinking up anything original or particularly individual. Not that most people who say, "That was a good sermon," don't really mean it—no doubt most of them do. But at least two factors qualify post-service praise:

- In a public line many or most people will say nothing other than general, positive things, certainly nothing intensely personal.
- If there is more than one exit, people who have nothing

good to say will go out another door. Essentially, post-service comments are like radio talk show call-in polls: they measure mostly the opinions of persons who already support the program or its typical issues.

These qualifying factors strongly suggest that pastors shouldn't put too much stock in post-service praise as a barometer of their standing in the congregation. Too many pastors who have been forced from their positions by threats of action, or have been terminated by church votes, might never have guessed how much hot water they were in if all they had to go on was comments at the back of the sanctuary.

Consequently, a congregation's evaluation of the Sunday sermon really does not constitute significant feedback from pew to pastor about how church members really feel. Pastors need more than that. All too frequently, they don't get it.

Words of appreciation are usually spoken at the door of a home where the pastor has made a visit. But not even these remarks, though they may be more private and personal, are a sufficient source of feedback. How many people, even if they don't particularly like the pastor, are going to tell him after he visits them when there has been a death in the family, "I don't appreciate your coming: don't bother to call again"? Most of us are polite enough to say, "thank you," if thanks is due, even to people we cannot stand.

The feedback a pastor needs from people comes in the

form of things privately shared without the least bit of coercion, and response publically demonstrated by the church.

*Private Words*

Probably most pastors have a file somewhere with things they have kept from their years at churches they have served. The file will have the requisite letter to call the pastor, bulletins from special occasions, and news articles. Here and there in that file may also be notes like these:

- *Thank you for that inspirational message. It's obvious God has blessed you with the talent of speaking and preaching. I was truly blessed. Please keep me in your prayers: I will pray for you.*

- *God spoke through your message so clearly an answer to a prayer we voiced to God many times. I was at such unrest, and now the peace I feel is incredible! I came expecting a word and I surely received it. God bless you as you do his work!*

- *You have a refreshing spirit and influence. You have affected many of us in a profound manner. I occasionally replay a cassette of one of your sermons on eternal security—it's a true masterpiece!*

- *Thank you for being faithful through the difficult times.*

Such written valuations of a pastor's ministry help sustain him when the going is hard. God bless every member who responds to the Holy Spirit's voice and takes the time to write such notes.

Unfortunately, for most pastors such expressions are probably too few and far between. And sometimes they are simply too late. All but one of the notes reproduced above were written to pastors after they had left.

It is not uncommon for a pastor to go through a crisis with a church and for only a few people to know about it, namely the principals in the struggle. A pastor in a large, regional church told how one of the greatest tests of his ministry was all but unknown to most of his congregation. He and his staff knew, and the deacons and personnel committee knew, but virtually no one else did, though certain parties claimed to represent the views or feelings of the church. He said candidly that he believed that if he had let the general membership know what was going on, they would not have stood for the injustice being perpetrated by a few. While it was tempting to make the private struggles public, he added that it would hurt the image of the church in the community for it to be spread abroad that there were problems, and consequently it would probably hurt the church's outreach and its usual number of visitors.

One of the tragedies of this kind of situation is that people who might tell the pastor of their support aren't aware that they need to. But even when there is no secret about there being hard times, many church members who might regard themselves as being prayerful supporters of the pastor don't let him know. A pastor may come to a point in ministry at which he assesses his effectiveness as either being in a plateau or descending. One factor leading to this assessment may well be the absence of feedback indicating otherwise. Short of taking a poll or fishing for compliments, how is he to know?

All too often, a pastor will leave under pressure, gentle or otherwise, and only afterward discover through a mild flood of notes from members that they supported him and hadn't wanted him to leave. Where were they when he needed to know that?

On the other side of the issue, most pastors probably would prefer that private feedback from members also take place when feelings are not warm and appreciative, but hurt and offended. Most people in general, pastors included, don't enjoy the confrontation of being told they did something they shouldn't have, or didn't do something they should have. But one can't fix what he doesn't know is broken. The member who comes by to tell the pastor of a deep disappointment ultimately does him a favor.

Here's where the behavior of church members goes awry. Sharing deeply felt hurts is an act motivated by love. When people don't share their hurts, but hold them in, they are demonstrating a lack of love. Love says: "I've been wounded by you and you need to know so you can respond and we can be on good terms again."

Not confiding wounds is symptomatic of apathy, which by definition is the lack of love. Hatred would motivate revenge. Apathy, by contrast, is usually characterized by the absence of motivation to do anything, and this inattention to wounds contributes to festering and alienation.

Even when negative feedback does come, it may come too late to head off trouble. People sometimes say they didn't know how to say what they felt. But many times the late information is not owing to sensitive and thoughtful persons who wanted to spare the pastor's feelings. Instead, the pastor remains in the dark because the first impulse of persons who took offense was not to go to the one who they allege offended them, but to go tell their friends and people with whom they have influence. In many cases, long before they ever approach the pastor with their hurt they have reported their side of a story to a widening circle. If they turn out to be wrong about what they think the pastor said, or about his motives in doing what he did, or about his knowledge of a need that he didn't meet, the errant first report will have circulated so thoroughly that it may be impossible for anyone to correct it and undo the damage.

*Public Praise*

Both positive and negative feedback is frequently withheld when it should be privately shared, but corporate feedback is important as well. It is doubtful that most pastors would want to return to the days when churches went through a process known as the "annual call," essentially a review of the pastor's performance and a vote as to whether or not to keep him. But somehow the church needs to provide for feedback to the pastor—and the rest of the staff, for that matter—that will enable him and them to respond to justifiable complaints as well as to suggestions, creative ideas, and encouragement.

Even more important than a public or semi-public critique, however, is a church's giving praise where praise is due. Churches need to develop a sense of appreciation for their pastoral ministers and other staff. What is true of others is true of pastors as well: people respond better to praise than criticism, better to encouragement than to complaint. As the old saying goes, You catch more flies with honey than with vinegar.

Feedback is vital to the emotional support of a pastor. But other, more tangible support is necessary, too.

## Stingy Provision

Few organizations are as tight with money as churches. A few churches, mostly those with cultured, educated memberships, have a realistic attitude toward the support of their leaders, and pay them more than decent salaries. But vast numbers of congregations have an unwritten corporate policy of sparing their pastors the temptation of riches.

The principle underlying this policy, which finance committees may actually verbalize, is to pay the pastor as much as the average church member makes. This isn't a bad principle in general. But subjectively applied, it takes interesting turns.

*Forgetting the Golden Rule*

For instance, a certain blue collar congregation has an average income above the poverty line but not even in the range of the lower middle class. They call a seminary trained man as pastor, and propose to pay him a blue-collar level salary. It doesn't sound outrageously unreasonable, but two other factors color the proposal: First, most of the congregation aren't really happy with their own wages, and second, the church has six hundred members with no building debt, and could do much better by the man they called to lead them. Why aren't they blessing him more?

Instead, the members are paying the pastor what they wouldn't accept themselves if they had a choice. They have neglected to apply the golden rule. Actually, they've perverted it. While Jesus said, "Do to others as you would like them to do to you" (Luk. 6:31 NLT), these stingy members are saying, "We do to you as it was done to us."

*Inflating Figures*

Or consider a semi-rural church that pays its pastor a base salary lower than mill workers in its membership make, and then pads his pay with several other items which increase his check, but have mixed value:

- The pastor pays both sides of Social Security tax since the church doesn't pay a share as other employers do.

So the church may give the pastor a "Social Security offset" check every quarter. But he is taxed on this check just like anything else. Although the church calculated the check to be equal to what it would have paid had he been subject to withholding, the check increases his total tax liability, and thus reduces its own value to him by as much as a third. In addition, the church may list the offset check as part of the pastor's compensation, when in fact he is simply a buffer between the church and the IRS, passing on the entire amount of this "benefit" to the government.

- The church lists an amount designated as the pastor's travel expense. Such figures are, with troubling regularity, considered by church members as part of the pastor's salary. But they are not. Travel is a legitimate business expense. The pastor must account for that expense either to the IRS or to the church, and if he uses that money for its intended purpose it does not in the slightest way redound to his benefit. It is for the church's benefit. Travel pay is not salary. Counting it as such helps a church claim it is paying its preacher more than it is.
- The church has a parsonage, a nicer than average home they are all proud of, an edifice they built to help them attract pastors. For tax purposes, the pastor's salary includes a figure representing the fair rental value of the home. If the figure isn't actually added into his compensation on the church budget, finance committee members may verbally add it as they reassure

themselves about the amount they pay him. But a parsonage, for all its convenience and attraction to pastors in certain circumstances, amounts to a church's forcing its pastor to rent instead of buy. When he leaves, he has no equity in a home. If he serves a string of churches with parsonages, at retirement he has no house. If churches haven't paid him enough to invest and save so as to be able to buy a home, he may retire with virtually nowhere to go.

*Forcing Bi-vocation*

Finally, there are churches who virtually force their pastors to become bi-vocational. A pastor who works at a secular job so he can serve a fledgling congregation that honestly can only barely support him, usually does so by specific leading of God and with complete willingness from the beginning. But a church that is stingy with its pastor may force him to augment his income in a way that erodes his time or ability to function in ministry.

Churches need to understand the biblical reason they should support their pastors. The church does not pay its pastor to preach: it pays its pastor *so that* he can devote his time to preaching and the other ministries he performs. The church that wants to avoid defeating its pastor in his calling, and hurting itself as well, will give serious attention to paying him sufficiently to cast all doubt from his mind about his ability to support his wife and children and provide for his future and retirement, and to do so without just barely getting by.

Even if a church pays its preacher enough, it may never be quite satisfied with what he does. Members' dissatisfaction may be entirely the result of measuring him against others.

## Unfair Comparisons

As discussed elsewhere in this book, preachers often feel compelled to change their style or add things to their ministry or become something they're not, simply because they're trying to compete with the famous local or national pastors their church members have seen. More should be said about this destructive behavior of Christians in churches.

Recent years have seen an increase in the number of regional churches (churches that draw the bulk of their members from a wide region outside their immediate surroundings) and a dramatic rise of new, non-denominational congregations (which tend to be regional as well). While there have always been a few people in most churches who alternated between their own church and one where they had family members or friends, the burgeoning of these regional and sometimes "mega-churches" has generated an unprecedented comparison by church members. Because many of these churches have television ministries, their influence acquires the potential not only to reach the unreached, but also to woo members away from existing churches with even greater power.

For instance, if members take a notion to attend a

another church and feel led to join, that's their prerogative. If they go to a service on an impulse, not indicating an interest to join or be visited, but the church visits them anyway and actively recruits them, that's sheep stealing. But if these same members, while they may not join the church in question, come back and tell all their friends about how the community church does things, or how wonderful its pastor is, that's destructive comparison.

*The Style Game*

One of the chief areas of comparison is the style of worship. While people may pit any church or tradition against another, currently the greatest "competition" ongoing in the Christian community is that of "contemporary" vs. "traditional" worship. (Both these terms are subject to much interpretation, depending on who is using them.[2]) Though any church and any style of worship can be the subject of unfair comparisons, consider an illustration involving contemporary-worship churches.

Contemporary worship styles dominate among the new

---

[2]The term "Contemporary" applied to worship arose in the wake of the 60s to describe the musical changes attributable to the original Baby Boomer generation. However, Gen-Xers further altered the musical style and distanced themselves from the Boomers. To them, "contemporary" was already becoming old by the 90s. By the turn of the century, they were calling their worship style "Modern." Then came the Millennials. Now, even Modern is under revision. For our purposes, we'll settle on "Contemporary" as compared with "Traditional."

"community church" starts throughout the country. Many churches that have achieved regional status, both denominational and non-denominational, have done so in part because they purposely adopted the contemporary approach to worship elements. Pop-like, modern music dominates their services, and appeals not only to the youth generation but also to many adults reared in the 60s and 70s with folk and rock music as staple fare.

Vast numbers of these members with musical tastes differing from their parents' nevertheless stayed in their parents' churches and were relatively content to have occasional contemporary music over the years. But not all baby boomers are enamored of contemporary worship music, and most of the older members, retirement age and up, have no desire to replace the hymns that have become dear to them through a lifetime of pilgrimage, with choruses, or what may seem to them to be no different from the rock-and-roll stations they do not and will not listen to.

Pastors in many churches have adopted a "blended" approach to worship, seeking to please all of the people some of the time. For most situations this is the only wise course. Pastors have a duty to lead worship for the entire congregation. Changing the longstanding worship style of a congregation in an attempt to market the church to a new demographic group usually results in major conflict. Older, traditionally oriented members are often left out of consideration.

It is not the burgeoning of contemporary or regional churches per se that constitutes a problem for other churches. It is the behavior of Christians who have visited them and then return to try to make their own churches just like them.

What pastor hasn't gotten a sample bulletin from a "competing" church, and sensed clearly the implication that he should learn from it? Many members are not even so subtle. Most pastors are tired of hearing the names of one or two churches near them that do things another way, that have this ministry or that, that have this group or soloist or a praise band playing every other Sunday. Most pastors can identify several persons in their churches who actually attend the "competing" church between ten and twenty-five percent of the time, and then make that church the topic of a great portion of their conversation when they are at their home church.

All this comparison is rude, unfair, and thoughtless. Are there pastors who lack any sense of creativity, and could benefit by someone's sharing a few ideas from other places? Of course, there are. Are there churches that need to take into consideration the cultural flavor of their neighborhoods in order to communicate effectively with people who may visit their worship? Again, obviously, there are.

But are most pastors dolts who don't know how to organize worship? No. Do church members think that their pastors don't have a purpose in having chosen the form or plan of worship in which they are leading their churches? Apparently, some do think that.

Lewis Grizzard, the quintessential Southern humorist

who died a few years ago, loved to venerate Southern customs and rib Yankees about theirs. Grizzard said, "I tell 'em, 'Come on down here, eat our food, breathe our air, marry out women, that's all right, we don't care. Ain't but one thing we ask you to do if you've moved down to Atlanta from up north: we don't want you to tell us how you used to do it back in Cleveland. We don't care.' I always tell 'em, 'You don't like it down here, Delta's ready when you are[3], I guarantee ya!'"[4]

Probably most pastors at times would like to tell their members who continually go other places and come back to play the comparison game, "Don't tell me how they do it over there." Sometimes the frustrated pastor would even like to say, "Please just join the other church: you obviously like it better than your own."

Some people have always "shopped around" for a church. But observers of the church in modern culture have described the trend of a consumer approach to church selection as unprecedented. And often the "features" these shoppers are looking for don't have much to do with theological matters, but with style and conveniences. Some churches and even whole denominations have responded to this consumer mentality by developing strategies to "market" the church to its community.

---

[3]"Delta's ready when you are" was an advertising slogan adopted by Delta Airlines in 1968.

[4]Lewis Grizzard, *On the Road with Lewis Grizzard,* Southern Tracks STL-004, 1985.

The value of this marketing approach in any given situation might be debated; but what brought it on in the first place was often the willingness of persons to pit one church against another, and usually on the basis of factors not really central to what the Christian faith is about.

Are these subjects of chronic vexation simply a minor pestilence? Or do they actually help defeat ministries and destroy churches? Clearly they do. As feedback is withheld, as pastors are routinely underpaid, and as complaining comparisons spread—as they always do—pastors are undermined, churches are weakened and worship and ministries are trivialized. These contributing factors to churches' unrest and ferment aid and abet the work of the master adversary himself, Satan, as he attempts through every possible means to destroy the work of God by obscuring and deterring the saving message of Christ.

Are there any solutions to the myriad ways in which many churches in effect undermine themselves by counteracting and neutralizing the ministries of the persons who serve them through leading them in accomplishing the great commission? There are such solutions, as we shall see, if churches are willing to hear them and submit themselves to them.

# 11

# Sacred Solutions

**Do not conform anymore to the pattern of this world, but be transformed by the renewing of your mind. Then you will be able to test and approve what God's will is—his good, pleasing and perfect will.**
**Romans 12:2 NIV**

**If anyone wants to be contentious about this, we have no other practice—nor do the churches of God.**
**1 Corinthians 11:16 NIV**

**For God is not the author of confusion, but of peace.**
**1 Corinthians 14:33**

**He that hath an ear, let him hear what the Spirit saith unto the churches.**
**Revelation 3:22**

Churches often subvert the ministries of their pastors and aid in their own self-destruction by the means we have discussed in this book: organizational folly, traditional hindrances, and personal prejudices. If the solution to this subversion were to be found in concise, practical steps, it would have been developed into a program and taught widely as a quick fix.

That such a fix has not been identified demonstrates that it doesn't exist. Rather, the solution consists of proven, biblical principles, taught with patience, applied with insight, and learned with submission.

*The sacred solution to the epidemic of forced resignations of pastors and the corrosive effect of defective polity and practice on the spiritual health of churches is nothing less than God-sent revival for the church, and the recovery and reclamation of the biblical role of leadership by those God has sent to be their shepherds.*

## Revival

It is almost too obvious to say that the first, and perhaps overarching, solution is for a church—for churches everywhere—to have revival. Not *a* revival, but *revival*—deep, thorough, life-altering, mind-changing, heart-breaking, heart-remaking revival—is what our churches need.

Since we know or should know that revival is first and foremost the work of a sovereign God, immediately we should take a perspective on revival that it cannot be scheduled, predicted, programmed, or guaranteed. While God has given us numerous directions for ways in which to prepare ourselves for his reviving work, or has taught us how to put ourselves in the way of blessing, he has not given us any sort of "push-button" method of evoking his reviving work. And while he has given us certain promises connecting spiritual activities on our part to reviving activity on his part, we cannot control the timing, the extent, the expansiveness or the results of revival when his moving brings it about.

## Change of Life Needed

The apostle Paul instructed the Roman church to determine consciously not to conform to the pattern of this world, but to be transformed. The Greek word transliterates into our English *metamorphose*. Christians need to be daily rejecting ways of living that mimic the world, and instead to experience a "renewing of [their] mind" (Rom.12:2). Literally, Christians are to experience a spiritual metamorphosis.

The process of this change consists of the same things that conversion involves:

## The Requirement of Repentance

Many kinds of behavior found commonly in the marketplace, the office, the realm of entertainment, and in the relationships of the home, are worldly, not spiritual, and must be rejected. Every hint of unethical business practice must be abandoned. Every market strategy that makes use of deception must be left behind. Every kind of entertainment that nurtures sinful desires or impulses must be eliminated. Every way of relating to other persons that fosters resentment, creates distrust, discourages love, or alienates people from one another or from God, must be forsaken. Christians must take stock of their whole lives, confess humbly and completely before God their sins, from the minor, irritating habit to the most sordid involvement, and they must repent of it all, calling on God's power to change them forever.

True revival demands nothing less. And the revival that will change a church that is hurting itself and its pastors will involve repentance of the same kinds of behavior carried over from the home and business atmosphere to the realm of church life:

- Rejection of the pastor's leadership in the church is an outworking of a spirit of rebellion that rejects godly authority.
- Politicking and power brokering are at variance with the humility Jesus taught the disciples when he told them not to seek places of distinction, and these machinations contradict the principle Jesus taught that the greatest disciples would be the servants of all.
- Exalting tradition over biblical models for the church is precisely what Jesus condemned in the Pharisees' behavior: abrogating God's commandment by insinuating the superiority of some other obligation or desire.

Each of the behaviors we have described—the disrespect of the pastor's mission, the unjust double standards applied to ministers and congregations, the excessive expectations of pastors and the unwillingness of many in the congregation to shoulder any burden, the failure to honor the elder/pastor in compensation and support—and all the rest, are sinful conduct. They are not merely sub-standard activities that can be brought up to specifications through education, though Bible education will help. They are examples of sinful behavior of which churches need specifically and thoroughly to repent.

*The Value of Confession*

Once there is movement toward repentance in a church, there needs to be confession. In both personal and church relationships that can still be salvaged, little is gained by the claim of private repentance that is not communicated and confessed.

A pastor can show the humblest and noblest leadership by confessing his own failures. Most church turmoil in which pastors and lay leaders square off is touched off by some level of shared blame, including real or perceived inadequacies of pastors. Pastors must never pretend that they are faultless. But while they must resist the temptation brought on by burn-out and/or depression to admit to sins they really have not committed, they must be willing to own up to their weak areas of ministry and to commit themselves to the Lord's help in addressing those areas.

A pastor who had served a strong church many years

was asked to meet with an ad hoc group of church leaders about their growing concerns. He had served in several prestigious churches and had never had such an encounter. After listening to them describe what they believed was troubling the church, he agreed with them on several issues, including his awareness that he had exhibited a lack of joy and had developed a depressive spirit. He asked them to forgive him and to pray for him. His confession, which was not falsely self-deprecating, had the effect of diffusing the tension somewhat, and encouraged patience in how all parties dealt with a potentially explosive situation.

Lay leaders and whole churches, however, must also realize their need to confess. Sins of indifference, rebellion, and partisanship in the church are not private matters that go away when someone has a inspirational time in private prayer. They are public wrongs affecting pastors and other church members and will only be healed when church members—particularly including lay leaders—submit to the convicting work of the Holy Spirit and not only say to the Lord they are sorry, but also say to the pastor or other wounded members that they know they have grieved them.

Too often, what happens in churches where core groups of influential members have successfully pressured pastors to leave is that these persons have become heady with a sense of empowerment, and have not even considered their culpability in their church's turmoil, much less confessed such openly. On rare occasions an interim pastor who sets out to perform what is now referred to as "intentional interim ministry" will be able to lead churches to see their own faults and begin to address their weaknesses so as not to repeat the pattern in future church-pastor relationships. But how often does such a church contact the pastor they have wounded to confess their sins and seek forgiveness? Perhaps until church leaders who have shabbily treated the pastor God sent them have not only owned up to their sins privately but have also formally admitted to that pastor that they wronged him, their "misfortune" will continue.

In fact, the "misfortune" many churches fall into is a legacy of their own misdeeds. God uses such judgment to discipline those who wrestle against his will for his churches.

Since God disciplines those he loves (Heb. 12:6), even the turmoil and confounding disappointment of churches is often the proof of God's love: he is using difficulty to convince his people to open their minds and hearts to their sins, so they can repent of them, then confess themselves to one another, including pastors, and be healed (Jas. 5:16).

*The Urgency of Faith*

Repentance is not biblical, however, unless it is not only sorrow for wrong but also surrender to right—the conscious, determined commitment of individuals to God. Just as salvation requires turning in faith to Christ, so the renewal of a church requires getting its focus on Jesus Christ. From one perspective, it was getting its focus *off* Christ that got it in trouble in the first place.

If anything is clear in the New Testament about the

nature of the church, it is that Jesus Christ is the owner of it, the head of it, and the builder of it. Jesus said, "I will build my church" (Mat. 16:18). Paul wrote, "Christ is the head of the church, and he is the savior of the body" (Eph. 5:23 NIV). John's description of the churches in Revelation show an exalted Christ who tends and warns his churches as the one who has authority to establish them or else withdraw his life from them.

All this is elemental theology of the church. Yet it is appalling that in many churches lip service may be paid to the concept of Christ's Lordship while the church pursues a political model of control that sometimes looks like anything but Jesus. If a church is to escape the awful consequences of a legacy of power politics, it will be only by reestablishing a pervasive sense of the ownership of a holy Lord. This Lord is grieved by dissension and infighting. He is grieved by the persistence of pettiness and the plague of power politics. He is grieved by the many church members for whom church is about *their* desires, *their* accomplishment, *their* fulfillment, *their* satisfaction, *their* happiness, *their* families, *their* being noticed, *their* being in charge—in short, about *them.*

The book of Revelation was written in part to make the point that the church and the very world we live in are not about us but about Christ. The same passage in Colossians that proclaims the headship of Christ over the church informs us that the whole universe was created by and for Christ. It asserts that "he is the firstborn from among the dead, so that in everything he might have the supremacy"

(Col.1:18 NIV). The plan of the triune God is to gather all things together in Christ (Eph.1:10), and for the universe to bow at his feet and declare him Lord. It follows that the church, Christ's bride to be, should be turning its eyes to him, acknowledging him as Lord of its ministries and mission, exalting him as Lord of its worship, looking to him for vision, and finding him gloriously revealed in the guidebook he inspired for the church's faith and practice.

The sacred solution for the church that has wreaked havoc with its pastor's life and sown the seeds of its own destruction is to experience heaven-sent revival, beginning with repentance and confession, and issuing in a revolutionary focus of its attention on Jesus Christ.

How that revival will come, who will be God's spokesman of its great need, how the church will be led to repent, what will prompt it to earnest prayer, and what will take place to turn its eyes upon Jesus Christ—these are questions whose answers for any particular church are known only to God.

## Recovery

Revival is absolutely essential, and many good things flow out of such renewing experiences with God. Among them needs to be a second sacred solution for troubled church-pastor relationships, this one for the pastor: recovery.

## The Pastor's Recovery of Spirit

First on the order of business for the pastor affected by church turmoil and even his own ouster from service is the recovery of his own spirit. Fighting, rebellious churches struggling internally for power have broken the very spirit of many pastors whose only dream when they first launched their ministries was to be faithful to God in preaching and teaching his word and to lead churches to know Christ and make him known.

Contrary to the cynical assumptions of many church members, the vast majority of pastors did not enter the ministry because they were budding megalomaniacs who wanted to build kingdoms of their own. Most pastors simply want to be used by the Lord to build the kingdom of God. Yet along the way many a pastor has been foiled by a church that hammered away at his soul, chipped away at his freedom to preach as God led him, and filed down the edge of his message.

Isolated instances of strong resistance usually do not deter pastors who have a firm sense of calling and spiritual skin that is of normal thickness. But prolonged attack and constant antagonism to a pastor's ministry may result in profound discouragement. Whether or not church members engaging in this kind of obstinacy and defiance consciously mean to do it, they may kill the spirit of God's servant.

Ultimately, the pastor is responsible for his own decision to give in or give up. Minirth and Meier in their book, *Happiness is a Choice* point out with eye-opening accuracy that saying, "You made me angry," is placing blame on someone else for one's own choice to lose his temper.[5] But human relations are powerful factors in everyone's life, and while a pastor's loss of will to go on pursuing his calling boldly is finally his own choice, those who provoke that decision by wearing down his desire cannot be held guiltless.

In the midst of his despondency and sense of failure, however, the pastor who still has the ember of his divine calling glowing in the deep recesses of his heart must recover his own will to find and follow the will of God for his life. If churches are to find the sacred solution to the epidemic of destruction that envelops them here in the early twenty-first century, it will not be without pastors to lead them, pastors who have recovered their spirit to serve.

*The Pastor's Recovery of His Role*

As a pastor seeks a new sense of spiritual will and inspiration, however, he must also recover his proper role in church leadership.

An old definition of insanity is doing the same things over and over and expecting different results. Similarly, pastors cannot expect that merely redoubling their efforts to fit in with skewed, unbiblical concepts of the pastoral role, or to maintain a church's traditional but unbiblical arrangement of powers, will produce anything but the same

---

[5]Minirth, Frank B. and Paul D. Meier.(Grand Rapids: Baker Book House, 1978).

results: stunted spiritual and numerical growth, self-seeking partisanship, and simmering division. The pastor who serves churches caught up in such self-destructive patterns of thought and life must recover not only his spirit to serve, but his will to lead. He must recover his biblical role as an elder/pastor.

Paul's words to Timothy echo down through the centuries of Christian leadership:

> **Fan into flame the gift of God, which is in you...**
> **(2 Tim. 1:6 NIV)**

> **Watch your life and doctrine closely. Persevere in them, because if you do, you will save both yourself and your hearers.**
> **(1 Tim. 4:16 NIV)**

> **For the time will come when men will not put up with sound doctrine. Instead, to suit their own desires, they will gather around them a great number of teachers to say what their itching ears want to hear. They will turn their ears away from the truth and turn aside to myths. But you, keep your head in all situations, endure hardship, do the work of an evangelist, discharge all the duties of your ministry.**
> **(2 Tim. 4:3-5 NIV).**

Constant renewal of ministry gifts and motivation, faithfulness to the word of God, endurance and leadership in the face of opposition, forging ahead in the divine calling—these are the themes of these direct and challenging words from Paul. The pastor under fire must recover his sense of mission *within a biblical framework,* not by compromise with unbiblical tradition, if he is to be the leader and proclaimer God called him to be.

It will almost certainly be helpful for any pastor to go back in his mind and heart to the time when he became convinced God was calling him to ministry, and to remember the sense of urgency and purpose he experienced as the Holy Spirit worked in his heart. Years of training, refinement of his vision, and specific direction in his own pilgrimage of ministry may have filled in many details he did not have when first he heard God's voice inside his spirit calling him out to special service. But it is that fundamental urgency, that conviction of God's hand being placed upon him, that needs to be recovered.

An empowering understanding of the nature of spiritual gifts as described in the scriptures is that they are principally gifts of motivation even more than ability:

- **Prophesying** (Rom. 12:6) - The motivation to speak forth the word of God in exhortation and evangelism
- **Serving** (Rom. 12:7) - The motivation to minister to people in their many needs;
- **Teaching** (Rom. 12:7) - The motivation to study and present the life-changing and spiritually nourishing

truths of the Bible;
- **Encouraging** (Rom. 12:8) - The motivation to energize the despondent and reinforce the desire of people to serve the Lord;
- **Contributing** (Rom. 12:8) - The motivation to give, irrespective of the level of ability or wealth;
- **Leadership** (Rom. 12:8) - The motivation to cast the vision so that all may realize the fulfillment of God's promises;
- **Showing mercy** (Rom. 12:8) - The motivation to reclaim persons for fellowship with God and God's people, through forgiveness and help in their weaknesses.

The spiritual gifts described in 1 Corinthians 12 may be similarly seen through the lens of motivation rather than simply as a list of abilities. In fact, in that letter Paul comments that all the gifts he enumerates there are "for the common good," and he declares that though there are "different *kinds* of service" (italics ours), it is the same Lord who is behind them all, working through all gifts to do his own work. Effectively, this is a description of motivations, the urgency and prompting of God as it works through a person's own spirit causing him to want to serve God in a particular way.

It is these motivations that are the gifts that ministers must fan into flame. It is this driving sense of what God has put a person on the earth to do, this sense of identity that convinces a man that no other occupation can fulfill his purpose in life, that the pastor needs to recover or have renewed.

## *The Pastor's Path to Recovery*

The path of any particular pastor, like the process of any church into revival, will be individualized, because his own trek in ministry is unique. But the recovery of a pastor's spirit and sense of role and purpose in his ministry may typically include several developments or activities:

- A change of scenery may be a major part of God's plan to bring spiritual recovery to a pastor. Having a chance to leave an unhealthy church whose momentum may be impossible to overcome may be a divine gift to one whose own pilgrimage may take a parallel course downward if he stays.
- A sabbatical may fit into God's plan instead. A church may be only sluggish in its willingness to be led out of the bondage of its traditions, instead of being altogether unteachable. Its pastor's having sufficient opportunity to be refreshed and recharged may be the spiritual tonic for his own discouragement or paralysis.
- Improved relationships with other ministers in which perspectives, ideas, and inspiration are shared will clearly be helpful to the pastor seeking the renewal of his spirit to serve and his will to lead. Not just the few ministers everyone knows about who have been fired, but many, many others who have been through the fire but whose struggles have not been publicized as widely,

can share their experiences for the common good of pastors. Honest relationships with others who have been through the same thing has the potential not only to offer the consolation of commiseration, which can be negative, but also to provide the encouragement of experience that can make the difference between a pastor's giving up, and giving it his all.
- Doubtless, an intensification of the pastor's own spiritual disciplines—study of the scriptures, prayer, personal involvement in witnessing and discipleship, renewed fellowship with growing believers—will be a significant part of his renewal. Without an open flow of grace from God through the unrestricted channels of the heart, the rejuvenating, invigorating power of the Holy Spirit cannot restore fleeting spiritual energy or refresh depleted spiritual resources.

## Reclamation

While pastors may survive by periodic sabbaticals or stress management, it should be hoped that churches themselves can be reclaimed for their godly purpose. And while spiritual revival in general will drive the revived to seek and obey the will of God, having specific direction as to how to solve a church's difficulties will be immensely helpful.

Consequently, most denominational structures provide resources for help and intervention when churches become embroiled in tense struggles involving their ministers.

Though such events usually mean that the underlying causes have been around much longer, at least a church can seek help when troubles arise. Mediators are often available to sit down with pastors and churches and help them find a way through their crises. When churches take advantage of these resources, they may initially consider the process as a means of putting out the fire that immediately threatens their contentment. But along the way they may learn something about their own role in conflict, and the potential exists for lasting and significant change to begin.

Unfortunately, such resources often go untapped. A conversation with a man who was part of a team put together by his local Baptist association to offer a resource for addressing conflict—even before it arose—revealed sad and puzzling information. In two years of the team's availability, despite associational newsletter publicity and word of mouth to more than eighty churches, not a single church called on the team for help. Yet dozens of those churches were experiencing the internal ferment that took its toll on fellowship, attendance, and relationships with pastors and other staff.

*Delivering the Message*

The reason many churches have not sought help or intervention is not that they don't generally recognize they have a problem. It is that no one has convincingly delivered the message to them about what their problem really is. For many churches, the message they need to hear is that the problem is urgent, that it is not going away on its own, that it may eventually doom them, and that it is not a problem with pastors, community change or the economy, but a problem with themselves. As the comic strip character "Pogo" once said, "We have met the enemy, and he is us."

But who can deliver this message? Sometimes a pastor himself can deliver it, bathed in voluminous and efficacious prayer, saturated with the evidences of his own love for the church, and expressed with the greatest of care. But often a pastor abbreviates his ministry at a church when he attempts to address core issues of its attitude toward leadership, the dangers of power politics, or the perils of worldly approaches to spiritual mission.

More often than a regular pastor, an interim pastor may deliver the message. Especially those churches that have gone through a painful situation as a pastor left may be open just enough to addressing issues in their own congregation to let somebody new—especially someone temporary—speak honestly to them about needed change. The irony is that a church may let an interim say what it would not accept from its former pastor. But if the bottom line were that truth were heard, repentance were real, and churches were changed, few pastors once hurt in the process of that change would begrudge their former churches the experience of renewal.

Denominational leaders certainly play a role in alerting churches to their needs. Among Baptists and other congregationally governed churches, perhaps denominational representatives could say and do more to inject that message into fellowships at the local level without violating the individual church's responsibility for its own spiritual health.

But in every church there is still another person who could deliver the message: a spiritually growing, insightful church member, concerned about his or her church's rightness with God and survival as a body of Christ, and willing to say, with both love and power, what needs to be said, so as to challenge the church to act.

In one church, that member may be an older deacon who has seen years come and go and remembers how the church was before something changed in its spirit.

For another church, that message-bearing member may be a devoted and admired Sunday School teacher, who cannot leave things as they are without sharing his or her heart to others until the tide is turned.

For still another church, the member who precipitates change may be a young convert, freshly in the fold from the other side, who from his un-politicked perspective and with perhaps purer motives than many others, speaks with a clarity that few can deny.

Whatever the identity of the spokesman, the one who bears the message to the church that its behavior is both sinful and self-destructive will be the one who himself first hears that message—hears it in the depths of his heart and knows it is from God.

That's why this book was written: so that someone, somewhere, will hear the message that many churches need, and that one church, or two, or ten, and perhaps many others, will change.

www.ingramcontent.com/pod-product-compliance
Lightning Source LLC
Chambersburg PA
CBHW031628160426
43196CB00006B/328